WORLD WAR II
LETTERS

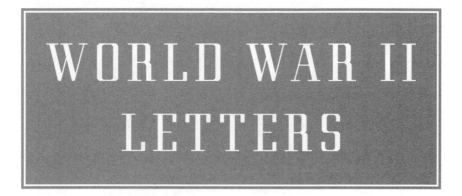

WORLD WAR II
LETTERS

A Glimpse into the Heart of the Second World War Through
the Words of Those Who Were Fighting It

EDITED BY

Bill Adler with Tracy Quinn McLennan

ST. MARTIN'S PRESS
New York

Dedicated to the men and women
who served their country
during World War II

CONTENTS

CONTENTS

PART V

Away from Home—Impressions of New Lands   149

PART VI

POWs—Life in the Camps   183

PART VII

Injured and Killed in Action and Caretakers on the Front Line   203

PART VIII

The End of the War   221

ACKNOWLEDGMENTS

Special thanks to Ginny Fay, Mary Nettleton, and Pat Ettrick of Bill Adler Books in New York, N.Y., United States; Bill Adler, Jr., Katherine Mansfield Slemmer, Jessica Smith, Nikki Collucci, and Jeanne Tyrrell Welsh of Adler and Robin Books, Inc., in Washington, D.C., United States; Carol Peaker in Oxford, England; Wayne McLennan in the United States and Australia; and Diane Higgins and Nichole Argyres at St. Martin's Press.

In the United States:
Patricia Fabrey and AWON: the American World War II Orphans Network (www.awon.org); Nancy A. Pope, curator, National Postal Museum, Smithsonian Institution, Washington, D.C.; Susan Black, the Eldred World War II Museum, Eldred, Pennsylvania; James W. Zobel, archivist, the Douglas MacArthur Memorial Library and Archives, Norfolk, Virginia; Larryann Willis, executive director, Audie Murphy Foundation, Orinda, California; Barb Turner, WAVES National Public Relations chair; Marcia McManus, U.S. Army Chaplain Museum, Fort Jackson, South Carolina; Lucile Wise, president, WASP World War II; Mae Nielander, curator, and Dr. William Oldson, the Institute on World War II and the Human Experience at Florida

State University, Tallahassee, Florida; Pete Wheeler, commissioner, Department of Veterans Service, Georgia; Nancy Marshall Durr, the Woman's Collection, Texas Woman's University; Stephen Plotkin, John Fitzgerald Kennedy Library, Boston, Massachusetts; Rob Hoskins, 461st Bomb Group Association; Toshiko McCallum, Hirasaki National Resource Center, Japanese-American National Museum, California; Arnold Hendrix, editor, *Danville Register and Bee*, Danville, Virginia; Sylvain Bellenger; John Earl Haynes, Library of Congress; John M. Purdy, director, Patton Museum of Cavalry and Armor; Justin Taylan, World War II Pacific Wreck Database; Margaret Vining, museum specialist, Armed Forces Collections, Division of the History of Technology; Monika Serester, Culture and Public Affairs officer, Australian Consulate General, New York; George Kilzer, consul, Austrian Consulate General, New York; Steve Robinson, director/producer of *War Letters* for Nebraska Public Radio Network; Fred Riley, 356th Bomber Group; Martin A. Markley, president, Society of the 3rd Infantry Division, U.S. Army; James Amor, editor of *The Golden Acorn News* for the 87th Infantry Division Association; Michael J. Horn, editor of *The Dragon* for the Fifteenth Infantry Regiment Association; S. Sgt. Pamela S. Smith, editor for *Airlift Dispatch*, 437th Airlift Wing Public Affairs; Art Giberson, managing editor of *Gosport*; Jane McHugh, *The Army Times;* Anne B. Adams, syndicated columnist; Claire Lyn Saxon, National Military Family Association; *The Oversear*, the publication of the American Red Cross Overseas Association (ARCOA); Sarah J. Rittgers, museum specialist, Division of the History of Technology, Armed Forces Collections; Steve Dixon, 70th Infantry Division, Tamara ("Toni") Horodysky, U.S. Merchant Marines webmaster; Rolf G. Wilmink, 75th Division Veterans Association; Richard Heller, the Society of the 3rd Infantry Division, U.S. Army; Lt. Col. USMC (Ret.) Robin Higgins, executive director, Florida Department of Veterans' Affairs; Pete Clark, Tenth Mountain Division Association; Barbara Walton and Debbie Gemar, Tenth Mountain Division Association,

Western History/Genealogy Department, the Denver Public Library; Dave McComb, webmaster of the U.S.S. *Nicholas* site; Betty H. Carter, university archivist, Jackson Library, University of North Carolina at Greensboro; Mary L. Linscome, archivist, University of Northern Colorado-Greeley; Dennis M. Pilny, newsletter editor of U.S.S. *Mount McKinley* Association; Glen Walker, Association of Third Armored Division Veterans and Museum; Herbert L. Pankratz, archivist at Eisenhower Library; Peter Branton, 104th Infantry Division; David Lippmann; Jack Valenti and Scott Miller, Long Range Desert Group Preservation Society; Jim Hanson, vice president, South 70th Infantry Division Association; John B. McBurney, D Company, Thirteenth Infantry Regiment, 8th Infantry Division; Fred Clinton, 63rd Infantry Division Association.

Throughout the world:
Roderick Suddaby, the keeper of the Department of Documents, archivists, Amanda Mason, Anthony Richards, Simon Robbins, and Stephen Walton, and archive assistant, Wendy Lutterloch at the Imperial War Museum in London, England; the Honourable George Baker, P.C., M.P., minister of Veterans Affairs, Canada; James Longworth, Ministry of Defence, Army Historical Branch, England; Dr. Peter H. Liddle, director, the Second World War Experience Center, England; Erica Levy, *The Age,* Melbourne, Australia; Sandy Vulin, *The International Herald Tribune;* Merilyn Minell, National Archives of Australia; Marcelle Bellenger in Caen, France; Gideon Junge, *Experience Holland* Web site at www.experienceholland.com; Paul Haget, Le chef du bureau de la documentation des études et des publications, Ministère de la Défense, Paris; Dr. Stephen Davis, project director, the Canadian Letters and Images Project; Regina Kölsch, Frankfurter Rundschau; Margaret Lewis, Australian War Memorial, Canberra, Australia; Kerry Blackburn, branch head, Commemorations, Commonwealth Department of Veterans' Affairs, Australian Capital Territory, Australia; Alex

V. Naida, webmaster of Front Letters; Rosemary Roth, R.A.A.F. Public Information, Department of Defence, Canberra, Australia; J. K. Maepufor, head archivist, Reference, National Archives of New Zealand; Jan Zdiarsky, Air-Historical Association Kovarska, Czech Republic; Graham Wilson, federal secretary, Military Historical Society of Australia; Neil Keene, Keith Kelly, *The Galway Advertiser* in Ireland; *Wings,* the journal of the Royal Australian Air Force Association; Eric Reits, Panzer Page; Peter Krans of Documentatiegroep '40–'45 in the Netherlands.

FROM THE EDITORS

Grammatical and spelling errors have been corrected in the following letters to make them easier to read; however, in some letters these errors were intentionally left unchanged to retain the voice of the authors.

Depending on the writer's nationality, spelling and punctuation are consistent either with American standards or, in the case of British or Commonwealth writers, with British standards.

Ellipses are used to indicate where a passage has been omitted by the editors. These sections usually contain personal information relating to family members at home, and their removal does not take away from the overall content of the letter. Some of the letters are excerpts from the originals and are identified as such.

The word "censored" in brackets indicates where the government censor deleted sections of letters. In some cases, the censor has written directly on a letter, such as "Address deleted by Censor," which has not been omitted.

Where possible, biographical information about the letter writer introduces the correspondence. In some instances, little is known about the writer. Each letter writer is identified with the highest rank he or she achieved upon leaving the service, which was not necessarily his or her rank at the time of writing the letter.

This collection aims to present a view of the war through the original writings of members of both the Allied and the Axis forces. To that end, the editors have not censored the letters and hope they offer an unbiased look at the lives and experiences of the servicemen and women of World War II.

Last, the editors want to thank the hundreds of families and friends who submitted letters for consideration. We are deeply sorry we could not include all of the letters we received. We encourage the holders of letters and memorabilia to donate these artifacts to World War II museums and document collections for posterity.

FOREWORD

Americans are fascinated with World War II. For instance, we have recently seen how popular movies like *Pearl Harbor* and *Saving Private Ryan* can be, the latter having been derived from a bestselling book. Yet, it has been over fifty-seven years since the war ended, and the youngest soldier or sailor to have served in it must by now be in his or her mid-seventies. Our national interest in World War II, then, is not just nostalgia for a personal past. What is behind our enduring interest in this war?

Could it be that there was a clearly definable purpose in fighting that war? It was a "good" war to fight because Hitler, Mussolini, and Tojo were, indeed, an "evil axis." They posed a meaningful threat to our way of life. All wars since then have been of far less significance. The Gulf War of 1991 was perhaps the most important to our well-being. Ironically, we strongly denied the very reason we fought it, which was to assure our access to the oil of the Middle East. We felt no necessity to deny our reasons for fighting World War II.

Could it be that we look back with interest on World War II because it was our most resounding military victory? Other than permitting the Japanese to retain their emperor in a figurehead role, we demanded and received unconditional surrenders from all opponents. In Korea we fought to a tie; in Vietnam we lost; on the desert of Iran we lost; in Bosnia and Kosovo we "won," but the end result is still in question; in the Gulf War we again "won," but Saddam Hussein is still bedeviling us; and now, in Afghanistan, we've been very successful in battle, but our political victory is uncertain. World War II was a black-and-white proposition, a war we fought cleanly and effectively against tough opposition and in which the result was decisive.

Could it be that most men possess a warrior streak that makes them curious about war? If not, then why do most boys play with toy pistols, camouflage clothing, and other paraphernalia of war? For those who possess the warrior streak, World War II has one great advantage: it is easy to identify the heroes. Such is not the case with the messy guerrilla combat of Vietnam or the high-tech wizardry of the Gulf War or Afghanistan.

Could it be that we instinctively want to understand how cruel and gruesome war can be lest we stumble into the ultimate gruesomeness of nuclear combat?

Whatever intrigues us about the war we waged from 1941 to 1945, *World War II Letters* is a unique new way of looking at that war. It does not describe the grand strategy of an Eisenhower or a MacArthur. It is not a gripping tale of heroic battles. It provides, instead, a human view of the war. It does grip us, however, as when we read what a soldier wrote to his wife on the eve of the battle in which he was killed; or, even more so, when we read the letter a warrior wrote to be opened only if he died, and we know that he did die.

This book contains brief biographies of warriors, but their letters to loved ones make up the core of the text. We find some who can write only of banal everyday happenings. There are others who eloquently explain why they are fighting. Still others try to interpret the military strategy in which they play a small part. There are amusing, bizarre incidents, such as when fighting stopped long enough for some Germans to give fresh chicken eggs as a reward to their American opponents, who had desisted from shelling a German hospital.

One of the most poignant tales is that of a Canadian Catholic nun on a mission to Japan that was interrupted by the war. She had been sent to an internment camp on the outskirts of Nagasaki. When the second atom bomb went off at Nagasaki on August 9, 1945, she did not know that a first atom bomb had leveled Hiroshima three days earlier. She describes what she could see happening in the distance at Nagasaki. This has to be a unique eyewitness account of what was to her a totally unprecedented phenomenon. At least, I have not seen anything comparable.

What this book does is put a human face on war. It allows the reader to feel the unavoidable fear, the constant anticipation of death, the joy of candy bars from home, the patriotism that motivates the soldier, the camaraderie that arises from relying on others in combat, the pathos of being one of only four survivors in a unit that started with fifty-nine, and the mundane concerns that are just there, like, "Please send me more socks."

As one reads these letters, it seems amazing that they could have been written at all under the circumstances. It is even more amazing that a military postal system could locate these individuals so as to deliver the letters from their loved ones—letters that were obviously such a big part of their lives, even while they were staring into the face of battle. One soldier wrote that he had "almost continuous malaria, kidney trouble and nerves," but that he worried about his family constantly.

Warfare is turning increasingly to high technology, and in the process is probably becoming more indiscriminate in who becomes the victim. Reading a book like this should remind us, though, that at the bottom line of war there will be human beings with human emotions and human lives at stake. *World War II Letters* is a poignant reminder that war will always have devastating effects on individual human beings. One thread woven throughout the book is the changes that war brings to its participants. One writer laments, "Will I ever be the same? I am a killer."

Adm. Stansfield Turner

PART I

The Battles

BY LAND

Born on May 19, 1920, in Battle Creek, Michigan, Lt. Col. Louis Laun of New York was a headquarters battalion quartermaster in the Fifth Marine Division of the U.S. Marine Corps. Lieutenant Colonel Laun was part of the first group of Marines to arrive in Japan when the bomb was dropped. He was a captain on Iwo Jima when the following letter was written, but he served as a reserve officer, not a career officer, for the war only. He was advanced one grade after his retirement in 1950. Lt. Col. Laun received the Bronze Star for his service. He later participated in the occupation of Japan. After the war, he worked in marketing as head of Labor and Public Relations for Bates Manufacturing Company, as advertising director of Burlington Industries, and as president of the Celanese Fibers Marketing Company. In the government, he was deputy administrator of the Small Business Administration from 1973 to 1977, a member of the Executive Committee of the Grace Commission on Government Waste, then assistant secretary of commerce for international economic policy. He was president of the American Paper Institute, the trade association representing the pulp and paper industry, from 1977 to 1986, and a member of the Helsinki Commission from 1986 to 1989. He is now retired and serves on several nonprofit boards and as a volunteer consultant for the National Executive Service Corporation. He currently lives in New York.

Captain Louis F. Laun receiving the Bronze Star for heroic action from Major General Thomas Bourke, Commanding General of the Fifth Marine Division. Courtesy of Louis F. Laun.

12 March 1945
Iwo Jima

Dear Marion, Eben, Jimmy, Debbie, and Eben Jr.—

Greetings from Hot Sulfur Springs, Iwo Jima. This is to report that this particular member of the family is still present and accounted for after a thrilling three weeks on this fascinating island. Am sorry to report, Jimmy and Debbie, that I have yet to get that Jap I promised you, but have certainly had the dubious pleasure of being potted at by many a Nip who must have promised his cousins in Japan the same thing. So far the score is even and neither of us has had any luck.

The cards I am enclosing were mailed to a couple of the members of this ill-fated garrison, and I thought that anybody in the family who is currently running a stamp collection might like them.

This has been a miserable battle for both sides—the Japs have an interlocking series of defenses consisting of thousands (I'm not kidding) of caves supplemented by hundreds (and I'm still not exaggerating) of pillboxes and blockhouses. Our division's engineers have already blown up over 600 caves in our zone of action alone. They hide up in these rocky spots with plenty of food, water, and ammunition, and can't be dislodged by anything but the individual Marine crawling in. Artillery, bombs, and rockets seem to have little effect, and tanks can't operate in the rocky terrain. Grand spot. The Marines on this island fought a super-human battle and the Japs one that is super-superhuman. I've never seen anything like the determination of these enemy troops. We're all praying for a banzai charge to get them out of these holes where we can get at them. Until we do, the campaign will only make more secure its already unchallenged record as the bloodiest in Marine Corps history.

Have been more scared, more mad, and more tired on this operation than ever before in my life. Have had many a close call from snipers, machine guns, mortars, rockets and artillery, but so far have succeeded in ducking the right way. My warrant officer got killed here about ten days ago which hurt pretty much—the infiltrating Jap sniper carries a knee mortar now rather than a rifle and they've harassed us seriously. Have had many interesting times moving supplies up to the front of the battalion— at one time got a little too eager and ran a jeepload beyond our lines, which is a story I'll tell you sometime. Everybody is doing all he can and I know we'll finish this up as soon as it is humanly or inhumanly possible. Without tooting our own horn, my hat is really off to the Marines in this one. I doubt, however, if this island will be completely cleared out of enemy for a month at the least, due to the abundance of places to hole up in, and these Nips are just masters at it. We take very few prisoners, and the ones we take are either unconscious, or so badly wounded that they can't kill themselves, or out of food and water and crazy. They just don't surrender, no matter how great the odds are against them.

Well, I guess I'll catch up on my beauty sleep—hope we get off this dusty rock of sulfur flames soon—that bottle of champagne you're saving would look pretty good right now. Room service is lousy on this place, and with the water shortage I've not bathed since Feb. 18 and have shaved twice. Yoicks—I look like something out of Mauldin.

Best luck to you all—my best to the Ruhms—and Happy Birthday Eben.

Love,
Louis

. . .

Rottenfuehrer (Squad Leader) Erik Andersen was a Danish volunteer in the Eleventh SS Freiwillingen (Volunteer) Division, "Nordland," named to reflect the Scandinavian heritage of its volunteers. His nephew, Kris Dunn of Florida, who contributed this letter and translated it from the original Danish, says his uncle was born in 1923 in Thisted, Denmark, a small rural town on the Jutland Peninsula, and became a farmhand who "wished to have a life of adventure and glory with the SS. At the time the SS was not seen in a bad light; they were considered to be an elite unit, fighting against international bolshevism. Back in those days Communism was seen as a definite enemy. The Nazis who were in power in Denmark were very socially forward-thinking in trying to eliminate the class differences in European societies that were dominated by the aristocrats. They had just fought a successfully orchestrated campaign in the west against Norway, France, and the Netherlands, etc. The Danes basically let the Germans conquer their country in four hours. So here we have this young man breaking his back on a farm in Denmark, [and] he made the decision to join the SS because it looked good—they had sharp uniforms, good equipment, slick advertising, etc. He went off in late '41 and wanted to go to war with the

Russians, who he thought posed a threat to Western civilization." This letter was the last one the family received. Rottenfuehrer Andersen was never heard of again. His nephew says that it is presumed that he died in Narva because of the big battle there but that the family has been fruitlessly searching for nearly thirty years for the facts concerning Rottenfuehrer Andersen's fate.

March 17, 1944

Dear Mother, Father, little Elsa, Per, and Karl,

I am sorry for not writing these last few months. We have been really busy with the Ivans. We are doing fine, it is tough, but we are holding them back. We know that this is a temporary situation to lure them out of the lair and then later on strike the beast at the neck in the summer months. We have the Tiger tanks and some Panther tanks and they are virtually unstoppable; the Ivans have good equipment but no trained crews. I know we will be knocking on the gates of Moscow later this year. The Ivans are real savages; they have no respect for life or death. Out on patrol the other day we came across a body that was mutilated, butchered and shamed; this is nothing new to me, but this time it was somebody I knew from training camp. They will pay for their destruction. Hitler has promised us that the war will turn real quickly with the wonder weapons. No matter how many tanks and artillery pieces the Ivans have, we know that we are better trained, more logical, physically superior and mentally superior to them. They cannot win this war; I know because we kill so many of them they must be running out of reserves real quickly.

Good news. I was promoted to Rottenfuehrer (Squad Leader) 4 weeks ago. I am very proud of my accomplishments and am happy that the SS has placed the trust in me to lead my men into victory. This is really a big step for me in my career, I know.

It has been a little over 2 years since I have been gone, but I feel like I have really grown up very quickly. I miss you all so much especially you, Else; you just turned 6, I know, and I am sorry I could not have been at your birthday party. I know Mom and Dad did something very special for you. I just want to tell you that when I get home I want to celebrate the birthdays that I have missed.

How is everyone? I heard that Karin married some grain merchant in Copenhagen; that is a shame; she was the sweetest girl in town. I was hoping to sweep her off her feet when I came back, but it looks like I won't be doing it anytime soon.

I never thought I would say it, but I really miss Denmark; this country [Estonia] is so damned cold, flat, and very war torn. Denmark is really a land of milk and honey. I was able to tell you earlier of the destruction I saw when I went to Berlin from the American and British bombers. It was truly depressing. I don't understand why they are hurting fellow Aryans like that. Don't they know that there are people fighting and dying here against the Red Wave of Bolshevism so they can keep their society intact? It really angers me that they are not helping us against Stalin. His own people don't even like him.

Well, Mom and Dad, I know you are doing a good job raising Per, Karl, and Else. Please don't worry about me. The war should be over by Christmas, when we get more tanks and aircraft here. The Ivans keep trying to break us, but they will not succeed; we will prevail. When the campaign is complete, I can't wait to be back home with you all. I love you all. Say "hi" to my friends and tell them that I am doing fine, though I sorely miss them.

With love,
Erik

• • •

Cpl. Clyde A. Richards was born on a farm near the northeast Missouri town of Canton, 150 miles north of St. Louis on the banks of the Mississippi River, on December 7, 1913. He served with Patton's Third Army for the U.S. Ninetieth Infantry Division, 358th Regiment, Company D, Second Platoon, as a machine gunner. His unit arrived at Utah Beach two days after D day. They were involved in a fierce battle at the Merderet River, just outside Chef DuPont and Picauville, France, from June 10–12, 1944, in an effort to secure the river's bridge. There Corporal Richards suffered shrapnel wounds to his back and neck. In the following letter, he writes home to his parents four days after his injury from his hospital bed in Lancashire, England. He returned to his unit on July 20 and was wounded again on November 16. After the war, Corporal Richards returned to farming in 1945, then became an independent insurance agent and real estate broker in 1950. He owned this business until he died at his home in Canton on October 17, 1990. Corporal Richards and his wife, now deceased, were married at Camp Barkeley, Texas, on July 31, 1943, and raised a son and two daughters. The son, Norm Richards of Missouri, contributed the letter.

Corporal Clyde A. Richards's wedding picture, July 1943. Courtesy of Norm Richards.

Dear Mother and Dad:

This is a wonderful day in England—back in England where I can rest and have a chance to get well again.

The past week seems more like a wild dream now than the real thing. It all seemed to start so sudden and it ended the same way.

I was hit by shrapnel Sunday, June 11, on the front lines in France. It struck me in the back along the shoulder blades and one piece struck behind my right ear.

Please don't worry about me for I am not seriously hurt and when I recover I will be in just as good health as ever. I am one of the lucky ones. After the shells stopped landing on us, of the dead and wounded ones, only two of us were able to walk back.

I can't tell you just where I was, but we were doing a good job. I have been in some of the hardest and bloodiest fighting over there and we never stopped going forward. The boys are still doing the same thing. The Germans are desperate, hard, dirty and good fighters, but they can't even come close to stopping us. They don't have the guts it takes.

I don't have much paper today, so can't write much. Oh, yes. As you can see by the address, I'm in an English hospital. They treat me swell. Don't worry about me, I will soon be okay.

Love,
Clyde

. . .

Drafted into the U.S. Army in February 1942, when he was thirty-two years old, Pfc. William Pellicore served in the infantry for Gen. Mark Clark in the Fifth Army for four years from Africa through Italy. Private First Class Pellicore's nephew, Jeff Caracci of Iowa, who contributed his letter, says: "While in Italy, Bill was terribly distressed at seeing the devastation and the poverty and hunger of the Italian peasants. He would gather up whatever food, especially large quantities of Spam, which the soldiers detested, and would distribute it to the families along the way. Bill also tried to deter the artillery from using church steeples as targets for shelling. On more than one occasion Bill would say, 'If you do shell the church, when you enter the village, the people will hate you instead of welcoming you with open arms. Instead, why not use the crossroad intersection in that area, and you will thus avoid, not only the destruction of the church, but the deaths of innocent people as well.'" This letter was written to Private First Class Pellicore's younger brother, Ray Pellicore, as he got ready to go on his tour of the Pacific. Ray Pellicore would later serve as a medical officer on a patrol torpedo boat in Australia, New Guinea, the Philippines, and Borneo. Private First Class Pellicore was one of six brothers who served during the war.

[Excerpt]

T/5 WM Pellicore 36321685
Hqs. 77 FA., APO 464
C/o Postmaster, New York

February 17, 1944

Dear Ray,

I got your ten-page effort a couple of days ago. It represents the best thing you have directed my way since the president sent his greetings. I suppose now that you've written yourself out we'll have another interval of silence.

Did you know that in foreign theaters the government, to keep down V.D., sponsors prostitution? Also, along the highway in [illegible] you see signs like this: "Women who invite borders create social disorders—take a pro." Since I've been in the army, I can tell you that I have been a Trappist in my glandular life.

The account you gave of your medical service was certainly vivid and complete. I think you can safely say that that the average doctor in two years of general practice doesn't get the variety you obtained in your internship. This background will stand you in good stead as time wears on. Do you suppose after you have completed the required additional three months they'd permit you to take the State Board? They might if they knew you were slated for overseas duty. Why not make inquiry? And while I'm on medicine, how did you get your assignment to the Cook County Hospital?

The days that lie ahead, Ray, are going to be for you the happiest and most fruitful you ever imagined, so make the most of it. We're proud of you and the record you have made. Give everything you do the best you got and success will be assured.

As I write this I'm in a rest center near [censored] for five days of relaxation—actually three when you deduct traveling time. This is where we get a complete change of clothing, and, what is more important, a hot shower. Because we have been so active, only five from our headquarters were able to make it this time. Our gun batteries sent many more. We had been expecting to be pulled out of the line and the whole regiment rested in one operation, but this arrangement eliminates that possibility. However, I prefer it this way. This is no heroic stuff, but it does seem strange not to hear the blast of cannons, shells exploding, machine guns clattering, and the eerie roar of the "screaming meemies," the German six-barreled mortars called Nebelwerfers. (I just re-read this last sentence. What would Nicholas Murray Butler say about the construction: awkward and clumsy?)

Since I've been here I have had a look [censored] and a few other historical and cultural spots. A sight I shall never forget is the [censored] constructed in recent years to replace an older church on the same site. We have a number of Italian churches in the states called the Church of [censored]. I'm not certain, but the Virgin was supposed to have appeared here, and a number of miracles have been wrought. I don't have the space to tell you about the church. Words can't describe its beauty. Mass there was conducted as you hear it celebrated in the states—as I saw it in Sicily and Africa.

With the exception of the first two weeks after our arrival, devoted mainly to re-equipping, we have been continuously at the front, and here we have been subjected to the most fearful artillery barrages of our entire combat careers. I can tell you that that day after New Year's a shell made almost a direct hit on my pup tent a few seconds after I had plunged into my fox hole several feet away. The net result of that experience was a shredded tent, strewn belongings, a bit of dirt and stone on my back and a ringing sensation in the ears. When the sky clears, the Luftwaffe pays us a visit. In recent days, however, the sky has been relatively free from enemy aircraft. Maybe it's because every time they appear the boys send up so much flak you can walk on the stuff. The real reason probably is that old Fritzie just doesn't have the planes to spare anymore.

As we push forward we leave in our wake devastation beyond anything you can imagine—whole cities battered to rubble. One town, [censored], featured in the news some time ago, looked like it might have been a pretty progressive municipality, what with modern shops and an electrically operated bus line; but our bombing and shelling, plus German destruction, has rendered the place utterly useless. That is what Italy is getting to look like as we inch our way to Rome.

News analysts, commenting on the slow progress, attribute it to long supply and communication lines. Such guessing misses the point. It has never been a question of supply, equipment, or manpower. All of our grief stems from the mountainous terrain and the rivers and streams. Conditions of this kind permit only a limited use of our armor. In addition, the Germans have dug in and it takes a direct hit to get them out. Every house in a village is a fortress. To neutralize this situation we simply level the place to the ground, sparing churches and cultural buildings when possible. For instance, in the town we have just taken after bitter fighting is a spared church overlooking the ruins—a tribute, of course, to the accuracy of our bombing and artillery. But sometimes this precision work avails us nothing, as in the case of a counterattack when the enemy flattens anything left standing. So every town gets a double shellacking: once [when] we take it and again when the opposition seeks to wrest it from us [censored].

. . . to take it without artillery support. The result was disastrous for us. Morale hit a new low. Soon after, we got word that the no-fire order had been lifted. Yesterday, I watched out Fortresses, Marauders, and Mitchells blast it. Hundreds of artillery pieces fired on it. Hitler's boys didn't think we'd do it. Our boys at the front are happier today.

Well, Ray, this ten-page matches yours. I may not always be able to make this kind of reply. For the time being at least I'll be working under more trying circumstances. I'm holding you to your promise of frequent correspondence; so keep that pen filled. So wherever they send you my prayers for your success and safety go with you. Take care of yourself.

Will

Censor's note: "a censor's bad dream."

. . .

Dr. Robert Andrew Douglas graduated from the University of Melbourne in 1939 and completed his residency in Brisbane during 1940. He enlisted in the Australian Army Medical Corps in December 1940. In October 1941, he was posted overseas with other reinforcements to join the Ninth Division of the Australian army in the Middle East. Letters to his parents that begin in November 1941 and end in October 1946 were found among his belongings after his death, together with many photographs. Dr. Douglas had two brothers, Jim and Hugh, both serving as infantry officers in the army, and two sisters, Bea and Alice, living with their parents in Townsville, Queensland, Australia. His son, Bob Douglas of Surrey Hills, Victoria, Australia, shared his father's letters from the Douglas family publication Battles Long Ago: Wartime Letters of Dr. R. A. Douglas.

25 July '42

Dear Mother and Father,

Since last writing I have taken up a position uncomfortably close to the enemy. I was touring about the battlefield a week or so ago and happened to run into the ADMS and he told me I would have to take over from the RMO of an artillery regiment who was sick so I was dropped off the truck at his RAP and he went back. The RAP is situated under a little cliff practically right on the water's edge and the blue Mediterranean splashes over one at times. It is in among the rocks and not the sort of place one would pick in peacetime, though tolerably safe except for a direct hit from a bomb or shell. Unfortunately it is close to a crossroad and there are 25-pounders all around, some in front and some behind. As you might imagine these draw the "crabs" and the enemy shelled us for a week, especially in the evenings just at sundown. It is a very nasty experience to be under shell fire—worse than bombs because with the noise of the sea you cannot hear the shells coming. The closest shell was about ten feet from where I was sitting in the RAP and a piece of shrapnel tore a great hole in the tarpaulin over our heads. Naturally after the first few days the place was well sand bagged. The first evening I was here there were wounded lying all about and shells dropping at intervals and life looked decidedly glum. Fortunately an infantry attack in the last two days has interfered with the enemy observation of our area and we are now able to take an interest in surroundings and count the shell holes and bomb craters about the place. The bombing was incidental and occurred every now and then; an Itie dropped his bombs fifty yards away in the water and gave us some nice fish to eat.

Things have been quiet the last two days and we are all getting very chirpy. When our guns shoot the enemy and he shoots back at us it takes practice to detect which is which in the general din. The trouble with these artillery regiments is that they draw the "crabs." I do not know how long I will be with this crowd but it is better to address my letters to 2/2 Aust. MG Bn as I should think I will go back there eventually. This artillery regiment has done a great job and have shot away an enormous number of shells. The infantry of course bear the brunt of the fighting and have fought splendidly though with heavy casualties. After the first Italian debacle Rommel brought all Germans into this sector, which is a tribute to the Australians. One cannot sing the praises of the Aussie infantryman too highly as he is a superb fighter. The Alamein battle is at stalemate and it looks as though Jerry is even more tired than we are. Anyhow here's hoping that the coastal strip remains preserved from the attention of the enemy artillery and dive bombers.

Hugh's battalion is, I believe, still in reserve but I have little opportunity of leaving my post to see him.

Hoping you are all well,
Your loving son,
Bob

P.S. I have a swim twice a day in the beautiful water near our rocks but always with ears well attuned and one eye cocked at the sky and our A/A guns.

7 November '42

Dear Mother and Father,

Received a batch of mail from home on the glorious 5 Nov when it became certain that what was left of Rommel's Africa Korps was in full retreat. Our regiment had just moved into a new position and that afternoon I was on a piece of fairly high ground and watched our guns moving up across the plain. Jerry's guns opened up on them and I could see their flashes and then see the shells falling among our moving batteries. One of the batteries unlimbered and opened up and Jerry shut up all of a sudden. Next morning we woke up to find Jerry fifty miles away hotly pursued by our mobile forces but leaving the Australians in possession of the coastal sector of the Alamein battlefield. Our infantry had such a clubbing in the attack that they were unable to take part in the pursuit.

We now find ourselves in the old No Man's Land between his wire and ours. There are derelict tanks and trucks scattered about and there were quite a lot of dead, both our own and Jerry's, until they were buried today. The ground is full of old shell holes and is littered with shrapnel and bits of equipment. It seems almost desecration to be erecting tents, i.e. if one is fortunate enough to possess one on such hard fought over ground, right at the foot of Tel El Eisa rise, contour 25, the clover leaf and all the other well known landmarks of unwholesome memory. One has to be very careful though as there are booby traps and mines all over the place. The Ities even attach booby traps to their dead so that when somebody goes and tries to bury them they go off "Bang."

We are fairly close to the main tarmac road and it is most impressive to see it chock a block with traffic going west. Great tanks of all descriptions on their scammels, guns, fresh troops, lots and lots of Air Force ground staff to occupy the forward landing grounds. At the beginning of July we saw a similar sight though with an entirely different significance as we came from Cairo to Amyria on convoy. There we had a terrific road block which held us up for five hours but what we saw on the other side of the road then were battered tanks and completely disorganized troops in full flight—Tommies, Indians, South Africans in hopeless confusion. The procession west goes on day and night and it makes one wish that one could take part in the chase. Our infantry have lost so many men though that we would not be effective as a fighting force until reinforced. It is a strange thing after so many months to have the war pass one by. They don't even drop an occasional bomb on us now at night and the only planes one can see are flocks of our own all heading west to new aerodromes. It looks something like the swarms of flying foxes we used to see at home. About two hundred yards away are four big 6" guns made at Skoda works Pilsen which used to annoy us greatly in early July. They were abandoned by their crews in the middle of No Man's Land and neither side has been able to drag them away for four months. They are very good trophies. There are several of his 88-mm guns here knocked out in the recent battle and some tanks.

The account you receive in the papers of the fighting is substantially correct as I can see by reading old NQ *Registers* when they arrive. The present battle was very well planned and seemed to go off almost without a hitch. It was very gratifying to find out that the main attack would develop from our northern salient which we had conquered after such heavy fighting in July. On a narrow front such as this Jerry had been able to build very strong defenses in depth protected by extensive minefields so that our mobile and armored forces had no chance of deploying without an infantry attack for a start to open gaps in the minefields. This attack coincided with terrific aerial and artillery preparation to batter his defenses and morale. The infantry then attacked and opened gaps in the forward minefields and our tanks got through into the open areas and played about. The idea was to completely destroy his soft skin first, i.e. his infantry etc., and then polish off his tanks later on. He put in some counterattacks as expected on a big scale and was of course still in range of our artillery positions and got knocked back with terrific loss. It was hoped that his tanks would come in to try and rescue his infantry but not many of them did this as they would have fallen into a nice little trap. After ten days of this mopping up process another series of infantry attacks opened gaps in his rear minefields and our mobile forces streamed out in hot pursuit chasing him along the coast road while other forces kept swinging in from the desert cutting them off at different spots. Once it cracked it was easy but the cracking process round Alamein and Sidi Abd El Rahman was very fierce fighting.

> Hoping you are all well,
> Your affectionate son,
> Bob

P.S. I believe Hugh is well and I hope to see him shortly.

• • •

Karl Friedrich August (Fritz) Fetköter graduated from the Friderikenstift Nursing School, Hannover, Germany, in 1933 and in 1936 joined the air force (Luftwaffe) as a nurse with the Air Force Medical Corps. In 1940 he was stationed at the air force base hospital in Prague, Czechoslovakia, to which the wounded were transported, and he lived off base with his wife, Ilse, and their first daughter, Ingrid. They later had another daughter, Jutta. His daughter Ingrid Günther Fetköter, who translated and contributed his letters from her present home in New York State, says her father later participated in the North Africa campaign under Rommel in 1942 as a noncommissioned officer (Feldwebel) surgical nurse assigned to the field hospital operating room, then moved to Corsica and Sardinia and finally continued moving north. At the end of the war he retrained as a ground soldier as all men were needed to fight the war. The following letter was written during one week in April 1945 in which he became involved in heavy fighting near Königsbrück just north of Dresden and had to lead 120 adolescent boys in a desperate attempt to win. On April 21, 1945, he was wounded, then treated in a number of different field hospitals. The last hospital was in Böhmisch Leipa, Czechoslovakia, from which he was released on May 8, 1945, and taken as a prisoner of war by the Americans to the camp in Marienbad, Czechoslovakia. He spent a few weeks in the camp and was released on May 31, 1945. His unit at the time of release, according to the POW papers, was 5. Panzer Grenadier Ersatz u. Ausbildungs Batalion

413 or Tanker grenadier replacement and training battalion 413. After the war he founded an all-male nursing school at the university in Göttingen, where veteran medics from the war were retrained.

Nurse Karl Friedrich August "Fritz" Fetköter
with daughter on home leave in Prague 1944.
Courtesy of Ingrid G. Fetköter.

9 April 1945, 20:40 hour

My dear Ilse,

Someone in our quarter is playing folksongs from home with an accordion and we are crying bitter tears. It was announced that the enemy is near Höxter and South of Göttingen. How is it with you and Ingrid and everyone in Göttingen and Lauenförde? If I just knew you are as well as I am right now, I would be the happiest person on earth.

We are now in a waiting position and up to now have had no enemy contact. I got together with a comrade and, should something happen to either of us, we would bring the news and whatever there is of valuables to the families.

Should my heart stop, it always beats for you, Held its love for you inside in faithfulness, Joined to you in tough and happy hours.

13 April 1945, 16:30 hour

On the 10th came the news that after heavy fighting Göttingen fell; how does it look there? Are you still healthy? For the last two days we are in position; at this moment I am cowering in a ditch, above us are low flying planes and tremendous banging; even with that, my thoughts are with you. Provisions actually improved, thus we are not suffering from hunger. Right now I have a bad hand, burned myself while draining hot potatoes; we also have to do the cooking. Writing is a little difficult right now.

16 April 1945

Since 5:10 early AM the Russians are shelling with artillery. I am back with the medical corp.

24 April 1945, 18:30 hour, Wamsdorf

My beloved dear Ilse,

Just today, as bad as it is, I get to continue to write this letter. On the 21st it got me, through the lower arm, which could not be medically attended to for two days. Perhaps you are in pain, too, and delivering [they were expecting their second child]. I must stop now, cannot continue, I had an operation this morning.

26 April 1945

Since I feel much better today and can now continue with writing, I hope by now your worst period is over. If everything went well and what we have will be a mystery for me, hope it didn't take too long. Even though I was in pain, my thoughts were with you all the time and how you were doing. The days from the 16th on I can hardly describe; they were just gruesome and I will tell you in person. Mostly I worked in the medical corps and had to remove many of the wounded out of the firing line. We were surrounded not less than three times. During the 3rd time, I lost my unit all together, that is they were dissolved. Then, on the evening of the 20th, I reported to the assembly camp at Königsbrück. There they gave me 120 men, inexperienced and about 17 years old. We only had 5 or 6 guns, and then bazookas and hand-shells, and most of them did not know how to handle them. Before noon we had to approach the Russians just at the eastern edge of Königsbrück. If we succeeded I do not know, because then I was wounded in my lower arm and had to leave K.

Marched for almost a whole day until I entered the field hospital in Radeberg where I received medical care. There I met a physician from the Göttingen Clinics, who just to calm me down said that Göttingen was not too badly bombed but that Northeim was. From Radeberg I was quickly transferred to the field hospital in Wamsdorf, Sudeten Province and for a few days now have received good care.

• • •

Lt. Marvin C. Weber served in the Third Army under General Patton in the Fourth Infantry Division, Seventieth Tank Battalion, Company D.

He fought in the Battle of the Bulge and survived, but he was killed on March 3, 1945, in Gondelsheim, Germany, during an attack on the nearby town of Prüm. His wife, Doris McCallister of Nebraska, contributed this letter.

Lieutenant Marvin C. Weber in Luxembourg, December 1944. Courtesy of Doris S. McCallister.

[Excerpt]

Somewhere in Luxembourg
7 January 1945

. . . We had a little incident happen the other day that might interest you. A Jerry officer came across the field with a white flag—they took him in to find out what he wanted. It so happened our artillery was shelling one of their hospitals and he wanted to see if it could be stopped. We sent two officers back with him to see where the hospital was located. While they were there the Jerries fed them a delicious dinner plus champagne, and when they were ready to leave the Germans gave them some fresh eggs to give to the Commanding General of the Division. You see, we never get fresh eggs and they were very sympa-

Lieutenant Marvin C. Weber in Luxembourg, December 1944. Courtesy of Doris S. McCallister.

thetic. Funny things happen in this war—it's very hard to believe at times some of the things that do occur.

I've seen a bit of action—the Jerries threw everything but the kitchen sink at us, and a few times that came along, but I came out okay. I got hit in the arm by shrapnel, but it didn't amount to much. Why I'm still around I'll never know, but I sure thank the good Lord. It's very cold here now, and [there's] quite a bit of snow. It reminds me much of Nebraska. The people here are pretty nice, and very pleased to have the Americans around. The news sounds quite good now. I hope it gets over soon and we can begin living like human beings again.

• • •

Capt. Arthur Care served as an officer of the Royal Corps of Signals attached to the Third British Infantry Division (the assault division) from 1941 until 1946. His letters from 1943 until 1946 were the only ones his family saved. They include descriptions of the training and planning for Operation Overload, of the landing on Sword Beach in Normandy on D day (June 6, 1944), of the pursuit of the Germans to Niemagen Bridge, and of the final advance to Hamburg. On April 5, 1945, Captain Care was posted to SHAEF, the

Supreme Headquarters Allied European Forces, and as a signal officer was present at the signing of the surrender at Reims on May 8, which he believes makes him the only person present on that occasion who had landed on D day. Captain Care now lives in Mount Martha, Victoria, Australia.

HQ 9 Br Inf Bde
C/o APO
18 June 44

Dear Ma and Pa,

Thank you very much for your letter of the 8th—mail is so welcome these days from home. I've very well, very dirty, and quite a bit tired. We had a copy-book landing, nae bother, and we've done all that's been asked of us so far; actually if you read the news in the newspapers you know more than we do about the general position, but take no notice of embellishments by special news reporters—they're all nonsense and they should be strung up. We got last Sunday's *Pictorial*—the biggest mass of lies and nonsense we've ever read. The BBC is very accurate in its news though inclined to be a bit previous; the capture and consolidation of a town are two very different things.

Normandy is a very beautiful part of France and reminds me very much of Surrey to which it is very similar. The people take absolutely no notice of the war going on around them; the Germans evidently treated them very well and they're not too pleased to see us; they suffered absolutely no shortage of food; we can buy as much milk, butter, eggs, bread and vegetables as we need. Actually, they've seen little chocolate, good quality soap or real tobacco, and we mainly trade by barter; they're very sharp and are doing very well out of us. I think the conditions are like this because this is a purely agricultural part; it may be very different further on.

Now don't worry; just watch that line move.

Love to you both,
Arthur

[Excerpt]

HQ 76 (H) Fd Regt
B.L.A.
19 Aug 44

Dear Ma and Pa,

. . . This part of the country has been well looted by Jerry before he left, and we are not getting the bartered supplies that we were getting—indeed we have had to feed the civilians now and then. This is the third type of region we have come through. The country-side is the same—farms, apple-cider orchards and cornfields—but the people have received different treatment from the Germans. The coastal people had been treated well and were almost active supporters of the Germans; further inland, although the people hated the Germans they had been reasonably treated by the Wehrmacht; those we are now with were treated brutally by SS troops who stole, killed and plundered all over the place, the pitch rising as their own plight got worse.

Most of the tales recounted are unwriteable; one of the less atrocious was the raping of a girl of 15 at the point of a revolver in front of her mother and father. In the well-substantiated fact that the SS men are as much hated by the Wehrmacht as by the rest of occupied France lies the only hope of deliverance of Germany from these thugs. If capture looks imminent they remove the SS markings from their uniforms as they know what fate awaits them if they should fall into the hands of French civilians; when they arrive at POW cages they are usually kept apart because many cases have been known of desperate fights between them and the Wehrmacht POWs. The tragedy is that many of these SS men were as young as 12 or 13 when the war started. Like all bullies, they are cowards, and when things go badly, they buzz off in transport, leaving the Wehrmacht to follow or die as best as they can. They will be a problem in the peace.

So the people here are terrified and very nearly destitute. Their homes are looted, their cattle shot, their horses stolen. In the farm here everything has been deliberately broken or ruined; and in a nearby farm when the poor refugee at last arrived back with the inevitable cart and hens he was seriously injured on opening a door by a Jerry booby-trap. They won't sleep alone and insist on sleeping with "les soldats anglais" even now. This terror is now turning to bitter hatred and the end of Germany with so much hatred against her looms terribly over the horizon.

The news is startling these days and we trust it will remain so, but so much depends on the weather that one can never say this is going to end until it is finished. We believe out here that they'll fight every yard till the bitter end. A cornered rat will do anything, and chemical warfare cannot be ruled out—that it would mean the ultimate massacre of the German nation by retaliation by our air power will not influence Hitler against it. We here are prepared for it, and would like you to remember that you must be too, as buzz-bombs could carry it, so please see your respirators are sound and handy until we have cleared the Pas de Calais. I don't want to cause alarm to you, but normal precautions are worthwhile and don't take a minute and give 100% safety.

This is all a bit gloomy when the news is so good, and it should be better I think before you receive this. We, that's Monty and me, have said this will be over by November, and we still think so—but that leaves us nearly 10 weeks, and many things can happen in 10 weeks. Just you keep praying for good weather and many of us will then be home for Christmas!

Give my regards to everyone.

Love to you both,
Arthur

[Excerpt]

[Approximately November 1944]
Address deleted by Censor
Date deleted by Censor

Dear Ma and Pa,

I'm afraid it's quite a time since I last wrote, a hectic and busy time too. What with the noise, the mud and the mines I've not known half the time whether I'm on my head or my feet—fortunately I've remained on my feet despite all three of these hazards. Mud—you've never seen such mud, even the old Jeep with chains on, with 4-wheel drive and in low reduction gear, nearly got stuck many times and did get stuck once. Once you get on a road you just keep going; the steering wheel is quite useless once you're in the tracks. And yet somehow, despite this and mines and shells and fanatical all-round resistance we've been plodding on, and for once have been head-line news and the tip of the arrow on the newspaper maps.

The Boche get madder every day; you just can't calculate what each individual is going to do. Many give themselves up at the first opportunity—one old chap even sent a civilian into our lines to say he was all packed up and wanted to go to England!—he was too. Others come over in organised parties 60 to 80 strong, while others run deserters' ferry service over some water. But not all are like this by any means; some resist fanatically until killed, some resist fanatically until they know the game's up then give in meekly; and then some go to ground and are a menace to everybody.

The last are very difficult to deal with—I came across one the other day in an awkward situation for me. We were going over a track when the leading jeep struck a mine and blew up; we didn't dare go round it or deviate from the track as we were obviously in the middle of a heavily mined area. A Jeep, by dint of going backwards and forwards many times, will turn in little more than its own length; so we decided to risk it and turn round; that was a nasty business in itself, it was made worse by one of these mad Nazis beginning to snipe at us; it wasn't a very nice moment. In the end 2 infantrymen went in for the sniper; he gave himself up without a fight, then sat on the side of the road smirking at us—you see, they're quite mad some of them.

They're on their last legs though, very definitely, the prisoners are for the most part very old men or very young boys; the former are relieved when captured, the latter cry like the children that they are—the better specimens, tall upright, fighting men, you very seldom see alive. How any human beings stand the amount of stuff we chuck at them is beyond my understanding, it's terrible even this end of it. . . .

Love to you both,
Arthur

· · ·

These postcards were written by Pvt. Adrie (A.W.) Koppenhol, who served in the Dutch army. He wrote the notes during the mobilization of 1939. The Dutch army surrendered after only five days at war because of the bombing of Rotterdam. Private Koppenhol's nephew, Arthur van Beveren of the Netherlands, translated the cards from their original Dutch into English.

Private Adrie Koppenhol's postcard. Text on postcard reads, "We have trained for a long time, but look, we're marching now." Courtesy of Arthur van Beveren.

October 21, 1939

Dear parents and sister,
I had a good sleep tonight.
We had to wait till 12 o'clock for a blanket.
I died from laughing.
They do a lot of funny things here.
Whether we could have old stuff they didn't say.

But you can send it though and some socks too because there are holes in them and a shirt too please because there's nothing left.

Best regards, A. W. Koppenhol
14th depot battailon

Private Adrie Koppenhol's postcard. Courtesy of Arthur van Beveren.

December 28, 1939
Wednesday evening

I can tell you I have arrived.
It was busy at the train station.
You see a lot of people when you arrive.

At least it is quiet today.

There are a lot of men at home because they're sick.

Nothing to tell you anymore.

Best regards and hope to see you soon.

A. W. Koppenhol

. . .

Capt. Arthur E. Hass served with the 752nd Field Artillery Battalion in Patton's Third Army. Captain Hass sailed aboard the Queen Elizabeth *on June 19, 1944, and landed at Greenock, Scotland. From there he went to Birmingham, England, and Abergavenny, South Wales. On August 18 the 752nd left Southampton, England, on an LST, or landing ship tank, and landed at Utah Beach, France. By December they were in Luxembourg, and they entered Belgium in January 1945. In February they entered Germany and crossed back and forth between Germany and France several times. Captain Hass's daughter, Joy Hass Stefan of Virginia, shared his letter and says it was written from the northeast corner of France, over the border west of Germany.*

[Excerpt]

Somewhere in France

Tues. Mar. 20, '45   8:45 PM

Hi Sweetheart,

   Two letters from you today—#249 and 250 written on Mar. 2 and 3rd. At that time I was in Bitburg, Germany. Surely was nice hearing from you again, honey. In both your letters you talked of moving and of having talked to Lydia on the phone. Of course your letters #245, 246, 247 and 248 give the details and I haven't yet gotten those letters.

Captain Arthur E. Hass with wife, Lois, and son, Eddie, in Brownwood, Texas, in February 1944, shortly before he went overseas. Courtesy of Joy H. Stefan.

9:10

Just listened to the news—sure sounds good, honey. Gosh, I don't see why those Krauts keep trying to hold out—they certainly have nothing to gain now. We've finally had it pretty easy for a day and have settled down to shooting instead of moving all the time—that's all we did yesterday and last nite. That's why I didn't write last nite—I was really worn out when we finally got into position last nite. Right now our guns are really blasting away—so much noise a guy can't hear himself think—I just hope it's killing Krauts. I didn't do much today—went back to Group hq. with the Col. after supper and got back before dark.

We're living in the woods again instead of in buildings in towns. I don't mind as long as the good weather holds out—besides the Krauts have been shelling the towns around here and it ain't healthy. This good weather we've had the past week has certainly been a break for us. It tried to rain today but only sprinkled a little. I got one of those new sleeping bags today—it's a dandy but I wish I'd have gotten it about two months ago during the real cold weather. This bag has a waterproof covering and the inside is 40% down and 60% feathers—they say they're really warm—I'll find out tonite.

I'm anxious to get some of your previous letters—you mentioned having called the doctor but that Joy was O.K. now. Gosh, honey, I can certainly appreciate your predicament—I just hope you'll keep your chin up and get along 'til I get back. What I wouldn't give to be able to be there to help you take care of the kids! Nine months ago yesterday was the last time we were together. It's sure hard to realize we have a daughter nearly three months old. One of these days this mess over here is going to end—those Krauts can't stand the pounding we're giving them forever—hope it's all over by the time you get this (I'm getting optimistic again).

Also got a letter from Tex today written Feb. 21. He drew me a floor plan showing how the office had been rearranged. He's sure a swell guy, and I surely enjoy his letters. Also got a couple of *Time* magazines and a *Texas Aggie*.

Guess I'll get to bed—still haven't caught up on the sleep I've been missing the past few nites.

'Nite honey—
I love you,
Art

BY AIR

The following letters were written by Maj. Howard ("Hitch") Brigham, who was operations officer for the 345th Bombardment Group (Medium), the "Air Apaches." The 345th flew B-25 Mitchell bombers in the southwest Pacific area. Major Brigham flew John Dos Passos over the liberation of the Bataan death camp, Santo Tomas, and one letter describes that flight. His story appeared in Dos Passos's book Tour of Duty, *which was published in 1946. He also flew the first bomber to land in the Philippines after the liberation. Another letter describes doing a hammerhead maneuver in a B-25; normally only a fighter plane could do that. The letters were submitted by Col. Bob Flint of Virginia for his uncle.*

October 29, 1944
"Somewhere in the Philippines"

Dear Dad:

Does that caption give you as big a thrill as it does me? Yesterday I flew the first B-25 into the Philippines; in fact it was the first Army bomber. It was certainly a wonderful feeling when the wheels touched the ground and we were in the Philippines. There was quite a crowd there to greet us as it apparently was a big event to see the first bomber come in. Some war correspondents wrote up the story so perhaps you'll see something about it in the papers. We have been paling around with some correspondents and army newsmen and have met several well known men from *Time, Life,* A.P., and U.P. It has certainly been an interesting experience. There have been several raids since we have been here but mostly single ship. A few bombs have been dropped but they weren't near us. The worst part of the deal is our own ack-ack. The guns make a terrific noise.

The way this all came about is that Bomber Command called up Operations and requested a courier ship to be sent up here. Naturally I grabbed the mission as it looked as though it would be an interesting experience. We had an uneventful trip up, other than a couple of hours of instrument flying. The fellow that came along as my co-pilot is a B-26 pilot who just got over here from 39 missions in Europe. His father was the third ranking officer, a Major General, at Bataan and so Jack (Jones) looked up General MacArthur here and paid him a call. I went in the General's house with him but did not meet him. It has certainly been interesting to arrive here so soon after D day. Also talked with some of the Navy fliers who helped work over the Jap fleet the past few days. The war has been livened up here lately hasn't it? Have we crowded the boys in Europe off the front pages yet?

I'm going to mail this at 920 so it will get to you faster but I thought you would get a kick out of a letter written in the Philippines. Because we will be flying out tomorrow you might well be the first man in Springfield to receive a letter written in the Philippines. Saying we are here has been cleared by censors so I hope if this is opened along the line nothing will be cut out.

Love

P.S. Will write again, soon as I get to 920.

March 28th 1945

Dear Bob and Fran,

When I returned from leave the other day I had two letters from Fran, one of which told of Dad's new illness. However, the one you wrote, Bob, has not yet arrived and I have received no further word about his condition. Naturally I am very worried but will just have to wait and hope for the best. My ten-day leave stretched out into four weeks and as usual I didn't turn out any letters. I wrote Dad as soon as I got back and hope that he is not too disappointed in me. Not that it makes any difference but when I returned my mail was not exactly abundant. None from Jinny, none from Bob and one from Dad. That's not very much for over five weeks.

Fran, you will be interested to know that I have met another one of your brother's co-workers, John Dos Passos, and we had quite an experience together. About the time our troops were entering Manila, we were asked if we could fly over Manila to see if the Japs were burning the town, which question was causing considerable speculation both here and at home. I decided to take the mission so off we went. We had a pleasant flight on the way up, circled the city and spotted only a few fires which seemed to be mostly fuel fires. Of course I had to buzz the place so we went tooling along just over the roof-tops, dodging smoke stacks and the higher buildings seeing what we would see. Everyone was milling around the streets in their Sunday best to welcome our boys who had entered the northern part of town and they all waved frantically at us. As we passed over Santo Tomas we saw quite a gathering and I decided to go back and get some pictures with our belly camera. Guess I'm just a newspaperman at heart. We went out over the water to turn, passing over numerous hulks of Jap ships which had been sunk mostly by Navy fliers, and suddenly there was a terrific rattling noise. Instinctively I started taking evasive action, which was rather limited because we were at about 50 feet but the noise kept up. Black smoke poured out of the right engine and I noticed a bullet hole in the left engine nacelle. I was all set to ditch her and I could not help but think if the LIFE board of directors could only see their John now they would like to hamstring me if they could get their hands on me. The right engine was putting out about half power but the fan kept going around so I gave up the idea of ditching, not being in the mood for a swim right at that particular point anyway, and started to climb. We leveled off at 3,000 feet and headed for Lingayen with our fingers crossed. The oil pressure dropped way off and the black smoke continued to pour out. Finally about ten minutes out the oil pressure quit pressing, the manifold pressure quit pressing and the prop ran away. For the benefit of the layman that means to turn madly, uncontrollably, at numerous RPM, like hell. I feathered the prop and we went the rest of the way on one engine (bless its little heart). After causing a red alert and a general furor on the radio we landed safely and with loud sighs of relief. After kissing the ground we took a look at the damage and found that two cylinders had been shot out and that about six of the cowl flaps were missing. It was the flaps beating on the sides of the engine nacelle before tearing off that had caused all the noise. That really had me puzzled and I was glad to find what had caused it.

As usual I had an excellent leave. We had a flat and a car and because we were down for so long we spent quite a bit but what the hell. Swam quite a bit, played some tennis and of course indulged in some of the minor vices. I'm fat as a Buddha—must be the milk and fresh eggs or could it be the beer. You haven't lived until you've had Australian beer. It is certainly far superior to ours.

Spent a day sailing on a 44-foot yawl. We had a marvelous time that day, perfect weather, good lunch, a swim and charming girls. That is the way to fight a war.

In my letter to Dad I explained somewhat about coming home. I have to sweat out a certain time after my promotion before my papers go in then it depends how long it takes for them to go through and after that there is transportation to sweat out, plane or ship, and so it is hard to set a definite date. Rather than have you all count on a certain time and have you disappointed I'll just say it should be this summer.

Fran, I started to read that article your brother wrote while I was in Sydney but as I remember I set the magazine down to join the mad rush to make beer call, which is very important. I'll finish it when I can find another copy of that issue. Dear brother, SWPA is not a branch of the service but means South West Pacific Area.

I am glad you were able to find a car and hope that you will be able to locate a satisfactory house. Tell Jinny that I am mad at her—not really but I would like to hear from her. Oh, I got the rest of my Christmas packages and thanks a million. Good-bye for now.

Love

• • •

First Lt. Joel Henderson Vicars, Jr., was born at Fort Thomas, Kentucky, and was employed as an asbestos worker in Lexington when he was inducted into service with the U.S. Army Air Corps, 524th Bombardment Squadron, 379th Bombardment Group (H), on April 11, 1942. He received the Air Medal and Oak Leaf Cluster for achievement while participating in five separate bomber combat missions over enemy-occupied Europe. He also received the Distinguished Flying Cross. First Lieutenant Vicars wrote the following letter home to his grandfather in Virginia, who had raised him since he was eleven. He married Doris Elizabeth Shipley on August 8, 1943, and they later had two children. After the war, he went to the University of Virginia and in 1948 received his bachelor's degree in architecture. Interim work took him and his family to Tennessee and North Carolina, where he started his own businesses—a fruit and vegetable supplier and an architectural firm. He died in West Virginia on August 14, 1972. First Lieutenant Vicars's daughter, Vicki Jung of Washington, contributed her father's letter.

First Lieutenant Joel Henderson Vicars, Jr. Courtesy of Vicki Jung.

[Excerpt]

Feb. 2, 1944

Dear Pawie,

Ground-hog day in England, but it is assured the little beast won't see his shadow at all today. It is mighty cloudy out today as is usually the case. We don't mind that in the least because it is at least a reliable sign that we won't make an operational flight over Europe today or as long as the weather continues in its present state.

I know you would like to hear about my flights but I don't suppose I'd better write about them; I'll tell you all about it when I get back. I've seen many things happen that are extremely hard to believe. I thought such things were dreamed up by fiction writers, but now I know some of the things can really happen. It is amazing and yet quite a common thing to see some of these amazing sights every few days.

In one respect I enjoy my missions, and they are extremely interesting. Often I look forward to them; on the other hand, the thought of these aerial battles literally scares me to death, but when you consider the small percentage of casualties, one becomes a bit more at ease. Our percentages of losses are really very minute, but when distributed over the entire 8th Airforce they are somewhat larger in appearance. 20 to 30 planes is an average loss per raid. 60 and 70 on some of the more rugged ones. However, when you consider that nearly a 1,000 bombers participate you can see how low the percentage will be. Our chances are excellent to complete the quota of raids. I am now half-way through. I should be home quite some time sooner than I had anticipated at least by late spring or early summer.

Our new crew is doing fine. We have a new place now, and have been assigned to it regularly. We are quite proud of the new ship. She is named "Big Duke." The new crew I have been assigned to is quite an experienced group of boys. They all have about 7 more raids than I do, but that is what I like about it. I'm no beginner myself. We get along swell together in the air, which is quite an asset. Our record so far is fine. We usually lead our squadron; right up the front of our formation, that is quite the place to fly in—plenty of fire power to back you up. . . .

Well, I must close—gotta get a little shut eye and some <u>rest</u>. Can never tell when they will come in around 3 a.m. to go on a raid. Loads of love to all at home.

Joe

• • •

Edwin L. Blanche, a Canadian naturalized in 1937, volunteered in May 1942 for glider pilot training. Already a licensed civilian pilot, Private First Class Blanche took basic and advanced training and graduated in December

1942. He was sent to Aldermaston, England, in March 1944 with the Seventy-third Squad, 434th Troop Carrier Group. He flew into Normandy on June 6, 1944, and into Belgium on September 17, 1944, during Operation Market Garden. As a second lieutenant, Blanche was moved to Bretigny, France, in March 1945, and flew into Wesel, Germany, on March 24, 1945, in the Rhine crossing. There he was killed during Operation Varsity. He was the father of three daughters, one of whom, Alece B. Egan of New Mexico, contributed this letter about her father's experience in the Normandy D day invasion, during which he piloted a glider carrying a load of nitroglycerine.

Sq 73, 434th TCG, APO 133
c/o P/M New York City
6/10/44

Alece Dearest:

Well, got back last night from the "big adventure," & got you, Mother & Bert off wires this morning. I do hope they got through quickly, but am afraid the congestion will be so bad it may take as long as a letter.

I know you must be curious to know what happened so will try to tell you without saying anything out of line.

I was lucky enough to be selected as the first pilot of the first wave of gliders. We followed the paratroopers in by four hours & landed while it was still dark. The long tow in darkness with a fully loaded glider (TNT & dynamite) was so darn nerve-wracking it was such a relief to cut loose that I didn't mind in the least it being dark, the fields small & full of obstacles & plenty of machine guns shooting at us.

We got down, by more good luck than management, in a small field, & would have made a perfect landing except for a small ditch across the field that took off the landing gear with a big jerk. No one was hurt & the load intact, but we had to jump for cover as a cannon was firing a few feet over our heads from the other end of the field. In the melee only a sergeant followed me to the woods & for an hour we hid out under cover.

We picked up some paratroopers, but they were going away from where I figured we glider pilots were supposed to go so I went off alone about dawn. It was so darn lonely, with firing in every direction, that I gave up trying to find our supposed headquarters & headed toward the nearest battle where I arrived in time to help about a dozen paratroopers clean out some Germans & take a few prisoners.

As we started out to tackle a village I ran into a Colonel who ordered me to stay with him & after various wanderings finally located some of the other G.P.'s & set up our camp.

We held the place thru the next night & about noon the next day started for the coast with a long line of prisoners, arriving at the American beachhead about 6 p.m. I was surely weary, no sleep for two straight nights & the long march with full equipment, watching for snipers, & at the beachhead I just dropped. We then had to wade out to a landing craft, up to my armpits & so after being changed from ship to ship, finally made it back to England Friday morning, & then by truck to the base.

The operation seems to have been quite successful, & I am so darn proud of our boys, especially the G.P.'s. They were afraid of nothing & pitched right in with the parachute boys. I can safely say that the Germans we met were no match for us, though we did not meet their best troops, many were just kids of 15 or 16 & there were a great many captured Russians & Poles.

I'm sorry I have no souvenirs—when I could have got some was too busy & I hadn't the heart to rob the prisoners (as most of the boys did). Please keep the enclosed flag, however; I wore it on my arm all the time.

My glider had a big Alece on the nose for the sweetest girl in the world, & I'm sure God brought me thru for you when so many of our boys did not make it. Out of the nine of us in this room, who all came from Maxton together, only two of us are back, though I don't think any are dead. I saw some of them near the wrecked gliders & even our leader was hurt pretty badly, so I feel I did pretty well.

So you see, honey, as long as we have control of the air, I am not in a lot of danger, & you don't have much to worry about. I never saw one German plane, so you can see we have them there.

I have your letter of the 30th & am sorry you had a long wait for a letter from me, but by now of course you have them all. I have written real frequently.

You must have had a busy Sunday on Confirmation Day. The kids are beginning to have quite a social life, with school, church & music activities.

The package was waiting for me, with a whole box of Loveras [cigars, his favorite brand]. You darling, how did you manage it. I will try to get some pictures as soon as possible now I have some film.

Loads & loads of love to you all, darling, I'm thinking of you always. Keep praying for me.

Ted

P.S. In case last letter didn't get to you advise when you get $320.00 I cabled last week.

T.

• • •

The following two letters were written by Col. John Wright Sewall, a member of the U.S. Air Force who was killed in action in December 1944. Colonel Sewall had been a prisoner of war at Davao, Mindanao, in the Philippines since 1942 and while being transported in an unmarked hospital ship (one of three) called the Oryoku Maru, *upon reaching Subic Bay, the Americans destroyed the ships. These letters were sent to his wife and were contributed by his daughter, Toni Sewall Mueller of Oregon.*

In The Field, Bataan
Feb. 18, 1942

Dear Eleanor and Girls:

One of the most painful things of this whole war is our complete lack of communications. If I could only get a letter to you, or hear from you, everything would be all right. When we left Manila we thought we would be back in a few days, so left many things undone. Since then we have been completely cut off from the outside world. Today I heard that mail was being started to the States somehow, so I shall try it.

On Feb. 12th I was promoted to Lt. Colonel, why or how I do not know. Living from hand to mouth as we are we do not even wear our rank because the Japs make a special effort to kill officers first. Shortly after arriving in Manila I was given command of the Group, increased by two squadrons, nearly 1,000 men & 100 officers. We never did get any airplanes and, as all existing airplanes on Luzon were destroyed in the first few days, and we knew it was impossible to get new planes, we set to work to train as infantry, and as infantry we have functioned ever since. We were issued rifles & all the accoutrements of infantry except machine guns. For machine guns we took our air-cooled aircraft guns and made tripods for them. We evacuated Manila by boat & had to leave all heavy gear behind. I bought a beautiful wardrobe trunk & stored everything in it except my toilet articles & one change of clothing. All that is lost to me now as it is in Jap hands. I have lost everything but what I stand up in, but so has everyone else. I have drawn no pay since the first of December, as money is not needed because there is no place to spend it. We are living in the jungle; no tents, just a mosquito bar. We eat twice a day, at daylight & dusk. Our kitchens are five miles to the rear & food is brought forward by truck. It is mostly canned salmon & rice. Morale is high & there has been little sickness. I have lost several men & one officer, mostly killed by bombs. The officer, Captain McCorkle, was killed in ambush while out on patrol. But we have killed hundreds of Japs too & have suffered very little ourselves. Yesterday we were shelled for nearly two hours, but there was no damage. We have foxholes & dugouts for protection. Fortunately the Japs have not shelled at night so we usually get our rest.

Every time I think of the Xmas packages I get sick. I bought presents for everyone. In addition I have written several letters to you, but airmail was suspended & so was steamer service so they all lay in the post office. Now everything is in Jap hands. But never mind. I will make it up a hundred fold.

How or when this letter will reach you I have no idea. I am putting it in the hand of God. "A thousand shall fall at thy side, and ten thousand at they right hand, but it shall not come nigh thee." Psalm 91:7.

March 3, 1942

Hang on to your hats, here I go again. Many letters I have written to you, always hoping that God will deliver them safely into your hands. Sorry, but this is one of my low days. Some days I feel quite cheerful & know that everything is going to be all right.

Depression usually follows an engagement when we lose officers & men. We are still functioning as infantry because we have no planes. Day before yesterday I sent Lt. Amron with a patrol of nine men to investigate a report of an enemy machine gun in a church steeple some distance from my front lines. He & his party crept up on the church, concealed themselves, but saw no activity for some minutes. Then Lt. Amron ordered a volley of fire into the church & steeple, but got no answering fire. After waiting some minutes he took one man, got across the square, and just as he stepped to the door of the church a machine gun cut loose from inside & he fell. The enlisted man grabbed him & hauled him down the steps, then he was fired upon from nearby houses & had to run for his life, leaving Amron in the hands of the Japs, not knowing whether he was dead or alive. When the patrol reported back to me, I immediately asked for artillery fire upon the church & soon saw it demolished through my binoculars. I learned later from artillery observers that a number of Japs were killed, but that doesn't give Amron back to me.

He was an excellent officer from a wealthy New York family, and had a half interest in Jack Dempsey's Café.

Yesterday, during a lull in the fighting, I decided to make an inspection of my front lines. I had no sooner arrived from my command post when a wave of dive bombers came over & let us have it. I was safely in a dug-out, but the bombs shook me from head to foot. After the dust had settled, we found one man dead & two slightly hurt. I am not telling you these things to alarm you. They are just everyday happenings, and of course war is a dangerous business. We thought it was impossible but the Japs are really giving us hell.

This is the hot, dry season & it is really something to sweat through. Now we are beginning to worry about the wet season due any time after March. We have no protection whatsoever. Tents are not permitted because of the impossibility of concealment. There are no surfaced roads & everything becomes a mass of mud. The rain is continuous day & night, everything is wet, matches become useless, leather mildews & rots and oh, God, why go on. Incidentally cigarettes are rationed four per day per man but they will soon be gone entirely. In spite of all this, officers & men are cheerful & optimistic & crazy for a chance at the Japs. It is well known that this is just a temporary setback & that when help arrives we shall push the Japs clear off the island.

I have learned the greatest respect for other branches of the Service. Why should we in the Air Corps sit back & do nothing just because we have no airplanes, and let the infantry & artillery take the whole burden? There is a tremendous job to be done & why shouldn't we all pitch in & do whatever is possible? Three cheers for the Infantry. . . . God is taking care of us & will bring us all back together again.

Your loving Husband & Father

BY SEA

Paul John Morrissey was a seaman with the U.S. Marine Corps in the Con-struction Battalion and was classified as a noncombat member of the First Marine Division when they landed on Guadalcanal. His daughter, Sue Morrissey Moore of California, who contributed the following letter, says her father wrote to her mother from a transport ship somewhere in the Pacific Ocean following the Battle of Guadalcanal.

Aboard S.S. Mt. Vernon
Feb. 13, 1943

And now at last I can write you a letter. I'm halfway home, expecting to arrive at San Francisco next Saturday. The ship is really majestic, a Queen of the seas, disdainful of space and the enemy alike.

And how did I get here, well here it is. I left Frisco July the 20th, and sailed for thirty days in what seemed to be an endless, aimless trip. The only break in this tiresome voyage was lying in the harbor at Samoa about 2 days. Finally we disembarked at Esperetu Santu in the New

*Seaman Paul J. Morrissey. Courtesy of Sue M.
Moore.*

Hebrides group. It was a pretty enough spot but practically uninhabited
except for the service men.

Meanwhile the Solomons held the interest of everybody. From what
scant news we could get all hell had busted loose up there. And we were
right next door. I recall with a faint smile, the picture of your hero in
full battle regalia on the first day of September, fighting to be the <u>first</u>
seebee to set foot on Guadacanal. I might have made it if I wasn't in
"D" company. However, when I jumped into the rolling surf and
waded up to the beach all the ham in me was bursting.

At last, to be on the battlefield for my country. This was really <u>it</u>. The
eyes of the world were focused on the little strip of sandy beach and a
cleared airstrip in a coconut grove dignified by the term "The Airport."
What an integral part of life "The Airport" was becoming. Before any-

thing else, before life itself, her daily wounds had to be patched, the steel plated dress of her runway set in place with inhuman speed. The mangled bodies of men were secondary to keeping alive the heart of the Solomons. The AIRPORT. We hadn't been there 12 hours when all the heroics and glamour were taken out of us. Oh, yes, sez I to myself, this is really it, but in a much different tone. From that day, until October 13, the incredible fury of modern air war was part of the daily routine. I don't say that to give the impression that I just took it in my stride. I and all of us hated it and were terrified of it. But it wasn't something you couldn't take physically. You had to.

The last clear thing I remember about Oct. 13 was getting your cookies from Wanamakers and sitting around my foxhole passing them around. The evening was growing late when suddenly the whole sky was on fire, the world was made of noise. A great scythe was cutting down the palm trees all around us. Little jagged pieces of white hot steel went through men's bodies so fast that they still continued to speak after they were dead. I remember it all vividly, and then again it's all so mixed up. It lasted until the 16th of Oct. when the enemy with his characteristic fanaticism finally threw the kitchen sink at us which Mrs. Jones had sold to Abie the Junkman who sold it to U.S. Steel who sold it to Tojo who must have had no use for it so he threw it back in a hurry. Well, the bastard missed me.

Anti-Climax. One quite quiet day I got this close to the shells from a 75 MM gun shooting down at us from the hills. I wasn't hit, just scared, and I stayed that way. So on Nov. 7 I was sent to Tulagi, a relatively peaceful island 22 miles away. Here I enjoyed almost continuous malaria, kidney trouble, and nerves. I worried about you all continuously and had a most miserable time. I left the Solomons Jan. 6, landed in Auckland, N.Z. about the 11th. I had a nice time and I think I'm all healed up. But I'm officially a patient and Lord knows what will happen when I meet the Medical Survey Board. The doctor in N.Z. thinks I will get an M.D. (Hon. Med. Discharge). I don't know whether or not this will be for the best. Right now I'm told not to worry, I am a casualty, a victim of "War Neurosis" and "Malignant Malaria."

• • •

SM Hubert Stanley ("Bert") Feben, an Australian from the state of Victoria, wrote the following poem in either 1943 or 1944. Feben was a nineteen-or-twenty-year-old signalman on the Royal Australian Navy cruiser HMAS Australia *in the southwest Pacific war zone. Already his service included time on the destroyer HMAS* Arunta *and a variety of assignments on HMAS* Australia *in hostile waters, the evacuation of Australian Imperial Force troops from East timor in January 1943, many convoy-escort and patrol duties between Australia and New Guinea, many bombardments of enemy shore installations in conjunction with troop landings along the coasts of New Britain, New Guinea, and what was then the Dutch East Indies, fleet patrols in hostile waters, and the attack on HMAS* Australia *at Leyte Gulf in the Philippine Islands on October 21, 1944, which was the first kamikaze attack of the war. This letter was submitted by his son, Geoffrey B. Feben of Cheltenham, Victoria, Australia.*

TO MOTHER

"Middle-watch" (midnight to 4am) thoughts of a R.A.N. sailor on "active service" during the 1939–45 World War; somewhere in the South-West Pacific War Zone.

> Oft at night when at twelve
> Far in the past with my thoughts I delve
> There is one person I always see,
> It's MUM the one so dear to me.

As the minutes of the night pass by
Thoughts of you Mum through my mind do fly,
As time goes and the clock strikes one
I think of you Mum with the love of a son.

I think of you tickling the ivories
And spreading those tasty gherkin savouries,
Of you cutting lunch sandwiches for me
When you and I used to dine at three.

As the clock ticks on and sounds off two
My thoughts are still of home and you,
And as I drink my mid-watch coffee
Reminds me how we mixed sweet toffee.

As time goes on and signals three
I think of how you fought and struggled for me,
How you, brave woman, saved those pays
To see me through high school days.

Then came the time, my school days past,
When I went to work and time went past,
And girls and cobbers were such fun
Due to the life you gave your son.

Then came a war with all its strife,
Upsetting the happiness of our life;
Although our ways are now far apart
Fond memories of you dear are safe in my heart.

When the world once again is in peaceful sways
And this war a vision of bygone days,

Then re-united at home I'll be
With all my loving family.

Then when at four off watch I go
I take these thoughts to bed below,
And think, as in my hammock I lay,
Of the time I'll be home with you mother to stay.

PART II

Religious Support and Strength

Sr. Regina ("Reggie") McKenna, a Catholic Sacred Heart nun, and her colleagues had been kept prisoners by the Japanese from the outbreak of the war and had been moved to the outskirts of Nagasaki in July 1943. Sister McKenna's nephew, Bill McKenna of Alberta, Canada, who contributed this letter written to his aunt's sister, Estelle Cuddy, and the rest of family in Montréal, says: "The atomic bomb dropped on the city on August 9, 1945, became a cornerstone of her tale of everyday life in captivity, so disturbed by this event; the letter has always been an important family story."

Nagasaki Internment Camp, Sept 12th, 1945
Japan

Dear Estelle and All:

A ring of the bell has just gathered the internees together to make the important announcement that four ships have entered the harbour. One is a hospital-ship and is willing to evacuate the internees tomorrow or the following day. The Protestant missionaries among whom we have been living during the last three years are the ones concerned. The Swiss Consul who came down from Tokyo about a fortnight ago gave them no hope of leaving for at least a month as the prisoners were to be attended

Sister Regina McKenna (middle) at Fuji Seishin Joshi Gakuin in Susono-cho, Sunto-gun, Shizuoka-ken, Japan, the school where she was working in 1968. The woman on the left is Miss Hori, a nurse, and the other woman is unidentified. Courtesy of W. D. McKenna.

to first. You can imagine the excitement in the Camp tonight. We who remain in Japan are all busily at work this evening to get letters ready to send by the travellers. They (the travellers) will be taken to either the Okinawas or Manila where their own Legation will look after them.

Now let me go back to the beginning of my internment life so that you may follow me better straight along to Nagasaki and the Atomic Bomb. When war was declared with the U.S.A. in December 1941, nothing happened to us in Obayashi except visits off and on from officials. All sorts of papers had to be filled in of course almost monthly, indicating our former residence in America or elsewhere and our reasons for coming to this country, etc. Finally on September 23rd, 1942, twenty of us were sent to Eastern Lodge, Kobe. Although we had a two-day warning we always thought that the Foreign Office would finally let us off or intern us in our own Convent. It was only a question of a fifty-minute journey on the train to Kobe, but once there, we were never to see Obayashi again. (Except once or twice during that year and nine months, a couple of our nuns went back to the Convent for about an hour or so for serious reasons, and always accompanied by a guard. This was only at the early stage of internment life.) The place where we were interned was a long narrow two-storied building, which had formerly served as an Inn for the employees of a large department store in the city. The meals were very good for war-time and it was due to a wonderful Japanese woman who saw to the ordering of the food, which was no joke under the circumstances. She was extremely clever and would do little kindnesses to this firm and that one in order to procure us butter, etc. When we were first interned, the house was already occupied by missionaries from Manchuria who were interned in their missionary country on the very day of the declaration of war, Dec 8th, 1941. They only arrived in Japan the following April and twice were on the verge of getting away, with their trunks even down at the harbour, but each time they were disappointed. They are the ones who are evacuating tomorrow to Scotland or England or Wales, and several are from the north of Ireland. Some of them have been in Manchuria for over thirty years, but they usually went home on furlough every six years. Four unmarried American missionaries left for America almost two years ago. The fifth person to go with them was a married business woman, a Southerner, but whose husband was connected with a large tobacco firm in Mukden, Manchuria. She carried on his business after his death a few years ago. I am sure she will manage to get back to the East before long. In order to make place for us in Eastern Lodge, several men and priests were sent to another camp. Shortly before our arrivals this lady was baptised and is now a fervent Catholic. Her eldest son who was in Shanghai was able to accompany his mother back to America. Well, to return to our interned life in Kobe, we and the seculars got on very well together. We had practically no place to walk, so now and again were taken to the hills for health's sake. We paraded along the streets two by two like a lot of schoolchildren and returned about two hours later. As far as our spirituals were concerned, we heard Mass on Fridays and Sundays when a priest from one of the other camps was brought here by a guard (from our camp) who used to fetch him and accompany him back. We were deeply grateful for this. I must say that the guards we had in Kobe were very friendly and we formed but one big family. When the five ladies from America left, the Canadian Dominican Father who had been saying Mass for us twice a week was sent back to our camp to take up his quarters again. We were all delighted as it meant daily Mass, weekly confessions and various conferences during the week and a most helpful sermon every Sunday. The seculars were very fond of him. He was gracious and friendly and always ready to put his personal interests aside to join them in their innocent games. We did a great deal of sewing and knitting and attended interesting lectures almost weekly from someone in the camp and profited by the musical recitals, etc. Now and again we had various kinds of entertainment. Everything regarding camp life has been highly organized with committees of all kinds.

One of our nuns was only interned a fortnight as she had an Irish passport and shouldn't have been interned at all. Mother Macfarlane (Mrs. Young's Sister) was allowed to be taken back to Obayashi about the 17th of December, 1943. She complained of her back and was soon confined to bed with a bad attack of sciatica. The Japanese doctor (who studied in America and, of course, spoke English fluently) was most devoted and interested in her case. But the Internment Camp was not the place for her. After a great deal of red tape permission was finally given to have her removed to our Convent. Of course she didn't seem so ill and the authorities knew how friendly the Doctor was with the foreigners so were rather skeptical. In spite of the best of treatment she received in Obayashi, she gradually lost weight and could do nothing to help herself. Her limbs grew weaker day by day and her suffering increased. Finally she passed away almost a year after her departure from internment life. Her Sisters must have received all the details from Rev. Mother Sheldon who almost through a miracle was never interned in spite of being a British subject. Mother Macfarlane died Nov. 21st, 1943. (We had already left Kobe for Nagasaki). Her death proved an immense sorrow to us all. She was so bright and full of fun. The children simply loved her. She was Mistress of Discipline in the Boarding School ever since her arrival in Japan about 12 or 13 years ago. She had a taking way with her pupils while, at the same time, she held firmly to the keeping of the School Rule. When we return to our Convent in Obayashi we shall miss her presence especially around the school part where she devoted herself day and night. She is buried in our beautiful little cemetery just a stone's throw from the playgrounds. Will you please express my deepest sympathy to the Macfarlane family? Mother Kate loved her Sisters dearly and was sorely affected when she received any sad news of their families. Please tell her Sisters that she was fully conscious at the end and was happy to go to Our Lord.

On July 1st, 1943, we were all sent down here to Nagasaki. The announcement of the removal of the Camp to such a distance simply stunned us. It didn't make so much difference to the seculars as Kobe meant nothing to them as all their interests were in Manchuria. But it was a blow to us because it meant all our connections with our Convent would be severed. We had almost a week to prepare and the authorities allowed our nuns, who were not interned, to come and see us several times. We left Kobe for the station July 1st, about 3:45 P.M., numbering 40. Sixteen were Sacred Heart Nuns, one a Sister of Naverre (English) and 7 Sisters of the Congregation of the Infant Jesus, who are all French Canadians. The remaining number were seculars. We knew we were destined for Nagasaki but had no idea as to how or where we were to be housed. We waited around the Station until after 5:00 with four guards who came from Nagasaki to escort us to our new Internment camp. We left the station, not so badly installed, occupying almost an entire car. It was a rather slow train, stopping at small towns all through the night. Passengers poured in with no place to sit down, but our guards roped off our part of the car so we were left in peace in our corner. We reached Nagasaki the following afternoon about 6:00 P.M. A bus took half of the party to their new camp. The rest of us stood in an open place outside of the Station, waiting for the bus to return. We had a good laugh over a funny spectacle. This is what happened. Such a crowd of passersby stopped to look at us that a policeman had to put a rope to keep the mob back. Finally, after a drive of about a quarter of an hour on the bus, we were invited to get out at the foot of a hill. We climbed and climbed up a narrow pathway through a pagan cemetery. Finally we reached the top and found a very poor wooden structure which proved to be a Franciscan monastery. Further on was a better constructed wooden building formerly a seminary but converted into a camp for men. Many of the latter left the country on the *Tai Maru* in 1943. The 16 men remaining were sent to Kobe camp as they wished to have all the men in one place. We arrived here tired and dirty, but fortunately all our luggage and bedding had arrived before us and we concluded that the good Polish Franciscan Fathers, Brothers and their pupils must have carried all that luggage up for us. We were forbidden from the very first day to speak to them. This meant no Mass, no communion. This building is a two-storied structure. On the first floor are classrooms. One has been used as a dining room, another as a common room and the few remaining were transformed into bedrooms for the married couples. The second floor is one big hall and at the very end of it [is] a nice little chapel. We found beds but nothing else in the way of furniture but plenty of vermin.

There was not a sign of a chair. Fortunately, we had brought our campstools along with us, which have since served even as washstands. The life down here proved very different from Kobe. We have all kept well from so much out-of-door life. There was a Chinese cook when we arrived, partly interned himself. His master, a Belgian, had been interned here but was sent to Kobe. The cook (although there was very little to cook) was often absent, either being sent on errands for the guards or in bed with bronchitis. So one of our Sisters has been doing most of the kitchen work. But teams were organized to peel vegetables, wash the dishes, etc. We did all the cleaning, washing of clothes, keeping the whole place swept, etc. We were often to be found on the hills cutting grass. Two of the Protestant Ministers devoted themselves to the precious cow for we were given some of the milk, almost a glass each, every morning to do us for the day. We kept watering it in order to make it last. Ladies and gentlemen were all anxious to cut as much grass as possible for the precious cow. I was charged with seven rabbits with enormous appetites. So you can judge that the life in this camp was mostly taken up with manual work.

We had few night raids during the winter months for which we were exceedingly grateful as it was bitterly cold here during the nights. But for the last few months, day and night, there were alarms. Cities and towns on this island were heavily bombed but not the City of Nagasaki until more recently. We have been completely isolated, so we'd had very little knowledge of what was happening. We had the daily news when in Kobe but once we got down here the newspapers were not delivered to the subscribers. Our kind Franciscan neighbors when passing the interned Ministers when in the fields would give them a bit of news on the sly. The Protestant missionaries here, and the Franciscans, struck up a real friendship. Of course the guards here didn't know that one of the brothers spoke English. Some of the Sisters here even did some mending for our good Franciscans and little messages went backwards and forwards. Thank God nobody was found out. We had Holy Mass on Fridays but never on Sundays as the Japanese Priest had to say Mass in his parish. Often we went several weeks without Holy Mass. It was difficult to accept this disappointment with three Franciscan priests living just a few steps away.

On August the 9th there was a "first warning" but by 9:00 there was an "all clear siren." I saw the Chinese cook go off to the city with the young Japanese woman who comes here by the day to do errands for the guards. Some of us went off grass-cutting a little later in the morning. It was a beautiful day. I should have told you that we are surrounded by hills. This will help you to picture me when the bomb exploded. One guard usually accompanied us when we went grass-cutting to see that we didn't go near the farmers' little fields but only glean on the narrow paths between them. Lately the guards didn't seem to follow us so closely on this point. Yet we were obliged to ask their permission. Having no radio and no newspapers, the disaster which took place in Hiroshima on the 6th never reached us. But we did remark on the nervousness of the guards. They didn't like to see us go any distance from the house; as soon as there was a "first warning" even those occupied with the farmyard had to remain indoors. At 11:00, as I was making my way down the hill with a huge bag of grass on my back, a heavy plane, although invisible, seemed to be moving very slowly just over my head. It was the first time I felt rather anxious about the approach of planes. I thought it strange that there was no siren as they have been so particular on this point. I think the approach of a solitary plane deceived the Japanese. I felt certain that it was an enemy plane. I looked up to see if it were visible, but quickly decided that it would be wiser to hurry back to the Camp as none of the others were around. I began to run. I had only gone a few steps when there was a fearful explosion and everything was of a golden yellow. It seemed as though the sun had burst and I was lost in its midst. I threw myself at once into a clump of young bamboo trees. I was lying on the big bag of grass. My face only felt hot. The golden light only lasted a few moments, but as I thought some more planes would be coming, I dragged the bag from under me and covered my head and back. As nothing more happened, I hurried back to the house only to find it had been badly shaken. Some people were cut on head and neck and arms, not seriously, and several among those who were wearing glasses got cut around the eyes but not one had their eyes affected. In fact it was miraculous I think that no one lost their sight because everybody indoors was in a building with numerous sliding doors made almost entirely of glass. The rooms on both sides of the corridor not only have doors made almost of glass, but for the sake of giving more light to the rooms, there are sliding windows on the corridor side, the whole length of each room. All these windows and doors were lying in heaps in the narrow corridor. Windows and transoms blew into the grounds and the chimney was found in a field some distance away in hundreds of pieces. Fortunately our Sister had gone out of the kitchen. Otherwise she would have been killed as the windows and glass doors blew in. It was impossible to get up the wide staircase as it was a mountain of plaster. We got shovels and made a little path up the stairs. The second floor, as I told you previously, is a big dormitory for the 23 religious and 4 unmarried missionary ladies. Some had the lens blown out of their spectacle frames, others had the lens broken, or cracked. Most of the people upstairs got under their beds as they are all near the windows, which smashed and crashed to the accompaniment of falling plaster. We had no furniture to be broken, but the bamboo sticks at the four corners of our beds to support our mosquito netting did look funny indeed standing out in all directions. The dormitory looked like a dried-up bamboo grove. We only have a space of about two feet between the beds. It took us nearly the whole day to shovel out the plaster between the beds. Glass was everywhere and all our little private things (mostly "empty" tins from the much appreciated Red Cross Boxes) were mixed up with the glass and plaster. The devotional little chapel was badly damaged and shaken. Statues were smashed and the walls and woodwork are in a terrible state. As the day drew to a close, we were all very sad, as the cook and Japanese woman had not returned. We learned that the cook had been killed. The woman died of injuries three weeks later. All the first day and night the mountains were on fire for miles and miles. Two-thirds of the population of Nagasaki are dead. We have not seen the city as we are hidden from it by a hill. We are just on the outskirts. The city itself is a mass of ruins. They are still burning the dead. No one is allowed to pass through what was once the city. From the second storey we could see buildings burning at the far end. We watched the flames creeping up to the pretty "Church of the Martyrs." Urakami, about two miles distance, hardly exists anymore. This place (Urakami) is the most Catholic part of Japan and possessed the most beautiful Church in the country. Families of even 8 or 9 children were all burned or killed. Priests young and old are dead. The hospitals here and elsewhere on this island having been destroyed, the wounded are not being properly attended to. Of the 10,000 Catholics of Urakami, only 1,000 survive. Our Japanese lay-sister in our convent in Obayashi, whose home was in Urakami, has lost her father, mother, two sisters, brother-in-law and nephew. Our 3 Japanese postulants have lost all their people. The Nuns interned with us of the Congregation of the Infant Jesus had many parish schools and kindergartens in these parts. All their houses but one are destroyed. Of their 14 capable Japanese sisters in Urakami, 12 have died and the other two will die also. Some were buried with their pupils in the schools. The effects of this bomb on the human frame are interesting the schools of medicine already. Some patients apparently recover then suddenly die from hemorrhages.

I must tell you how we heard of peace. We went to bed as usual on Aug. 16th—with our air-raid bundles close at hands although there had been no sirens on the 15th or 16th. At one o'clock in the morning (Aug. 17th), the guards rang the bell and sent word upstairs that we were to hurry to the dining room and not to take the time to finish dressing. No air-raid bundles were to be taken. This seemed awfully strange. We scrambled down in the dark as usual but found the light on in the dining room. A line of officials walked in, including our own guards, and ordered everyone to sit down. I personally thought that the Allies had made a landing and that the Japanese wanted to let us all know. The head man stood up and when all was quiet, smiled most graciously saying (in Japanese), "Congratulations! The war is over. We have been defeated and you are the victors." There was simply an "Oh!" and long drawn out "Ah" from us all. We were stunned. The official put out his hand and said in a jolly way, "Let us all shake hands and celebrate." Cigarettes and matches and wine were passed in abundance. Everybody behaved themselves and would like to have retired but the officials seemed anxious to have us remain on. We were supposed to be free from that moment but life went on as usual in the Camp. We hadn't had Mass that week as the Japanese priest who was accustomed to come had too much to do among his own suffering people. In fact, we haven't seen him since before the disaster. All intercourse with our Franciscan neighbours was still prohibited until Aug. 23rd, when we were allowed to go down to their little Church for daily Mass. Now one of the Franciscans comes here every morning to say his Mass and we can go freely to their Church for Benediction towards evening. We can speak to any of them at any time. The guards, strange to say, used to send for the brother electrician or brother carpenter, etc. to mend and repair things in the house all through internment life. Of course the internees got in many a little word with them by this means. As they had a radio, they managed by all kinds of ways to give news to the men interned. We expect now to be told any day to pack up and leave for Obayashi. We are longing to be back in our Convent.

I hope you are all well and happy. Much love to Lorraine and each member of the family. I am looking forward to news of you all.

Your affectionate Sister,

Reggie McKenna, rscy

• • •

Bishop John Aloysius Morgan was an Australian Army chaplain in the New Guinea campaign from 1944 to 1945. Bishop Morgan now lives in Canberra, Australian Capital Territory, Australia. His nephew, Rick Spillane of Essendon, Victoria, Australia, who contributed his uncle's letter, says he continues to tell stories of the war years. Bishop Morgan wrote the following letter to his brother.

[Excerpt]

HQ,
6 Aust. Div.,
A.I.F.,
(Wewalk Area).
20 July 1945.

Dear Frank,

Lately I have had to write a lot of letters for lads who have been wounded and to parents whose boys have been killed. So I find it hard to remember just when it was that I wrote a few lines to you.

Anyhow I have had a quieter time lately and am feeling pretty fresh again. Last week I was up into the Hills, but although the going was steep I enjoyed every minute of the journey. Father McDonald was in hospital sick so I had to get Mass to his Battalion. I still love the hills and [am] happiest when I have a pack on my back and am moving from camp to camp among the Infanteers who are doing the real fighting. There is a spirit in such camps that cannot be found anywhere else— and an atmosphere that is unique. Any physical hardship is well repaid by the companionship one enjoys among soldiers perched on some hilltop in a jungle camp. And they appreciate the opportunity of Mass and the sacraments. Last week about 30 natives were at Confession and Holy Communion at the various outposts—they act as sentries and guides for us and their work is very dangerous for they creep up to and into and through Jap positions. . . . Many of them—indeed most of them— know their Catholic religion remarkably well and from little things one can at times realize that they have really absorbed the Christian philosophy of life.

Last night I said Mass on the beach for some Infanteers who have just come out of the hills and who go back tomorrow. I know these lads very well for I was with them in most of their scraps. They came out last

Tuesday and have been given 3 bottles of beer a day for each man while on the beach. You see we get an issue up here of two bottles a week per man. These boys had been in the hills for months and so had twenty bottles due to them. It was grand to be with them. After tea they all came to Mass in the quiet of the evening—then afterwards in the moonlight they sat on the beach and talked and yarned over the beer till 10 pm. Being given such a little each day has meant they have drunk the beer quietly and sensibly. They just forgot about war and Japs and laughed and yarned together. They were all happier because they had fought so hard and done so well. It was a great couple of days recreation for them. Tomorrow they go again refreshed in mind and fortified by Mass and the Sacraments.

Well, Frank, these are just a few lines about nothing at all. My kind regards to Mollie and the children. I will write to Francis again next time that I have a few quiet days.

God Bless you all.

Alo

• • •

Maj. Louise R. Camden was single and enlisted in the Army Nurses Corps in 1942 at the age of thirty-eight. After training she served as the chief nurse at Sixty-ninth General Hospital, a field hospital, in Assam, India, caring for casualties from Merrill's Marauders, among others. Major Camden returned to civilian life and served as chief nurse at Veterans Administration hospitals in New York and Ohio. Her nephew, Rick Camden of Maryland, who contributed her letters, was born days after his aunt's return from the war in 1945. He remembers her as a woman of deep faith, dedicated to joyfully serving the sick and wounded, confident of her professional competence, and fun to be around. The second letter was written to her friend, Martha.

Major Louise R. Camden, Chief Nurse, 69th General Hospital (front row, left) sending nurses off to China. Courtesy of Richard S. Camden.

[Excerpt]

Letter from sea—en route to India 1944

Hello Family,

Greetings from the sea again—still on the way but hope to be someplace one of these days and when we do arrive I'll wire you immediately. So far I'm well and happy and we all have stood the trip, I would say exceptionally well. . . .

Everyone has been lovely—especially the Captain of the ship. This is the first time he's ever carried so many women, and at first he was rather concerned about the whole thing but the behavior hasn't been too bad and I guess he now feels we weren't too bad. I've been the

Officer in Charge of all the women and have tried to maintain order and discipline. . . . I guess I'm the only one who's been out on deck—just once—after dark—and that was a gorgeous moonlight night while we were near the equator. Never have I seen such a sight. The water was very still and the moon was up sometime before the last rays of the sun left the sky. We watched the colors of the sun change from all shades of gold to purple, red and pale pink. Then the moon made the strangest patterns on the water and for miles, as far as we could see. Far in the distance, on the horizon, the reflection on the water was such that it looked like a beautiful lighted city. The stars looked so close that one felt they could reach up and pluck them out of the sky. Until the sun's rays were completely faded, we could see the flying fishes, tiny silver fish, coming out of the water and flying, in great numbers, around about. Then when it was a little darker—at the side of the boat, we could see the reflection of the stars in the water. It was beautiful! The ship of course was darkened and it was a strange feeling to be way up high, gazing on all this beauty, in the quiet of the night. Would that all of you could have seen it. For me, it's been one of the highlights of the trip and something I shall never, never, forget! . . .

So far I haven't had a great deal of trouble—in fact no trouble in disciplining the nurses. They've all been grand and I've enjoyed it all. Did I tell you that one of them became a Catholic at the POE and another one is taking instructions aboard this ship? Naturally I made it a point not to discuss the subject of religion since I'm the Chief Nurse. I've been and will continue to be very, very impartial, however before we left the POE I suggested to them all that they take a day off—which I arranged for them to have—to take care of their own personal selves and see the chaplain—both Catholic and Protestant about any problems or worries which they might have and suggested they get their spiritual life in shape for the "Battle of the Atlantic." It was that which started the one on her way to being a convert, however, when she came to me—after she had already started instructions I gave her quite a good talking to—explaining to her that it was a serious step. . . . The other one, taking instructions now, is a college graduate and a very intelligent girl—older too. She had told me back at Camp Swift that she thought I was silly, thinking that God would even take time out to remember me let alone hearing my prayers. (She had seen my rosary on the dresser.) Then she also told me religion was for the weak and if my believing in all the fairy tales of the bible made me feel any better she thought it quite the thing for me to practice religion of any kind. Of course I didn't argue with her—but I did tell her in no uncertain terms what I thought of her ideas and asked her if she were really happy believing her way. Anyhow, I didn't discuss it anymore with her until we had been on the ship quite awhile and she came to me, with a Catechism, and told me she had seen the Chaplain, a Jesuit, and had told him she had had alot of time to think and observe and that I had something in the way of happiness that she didn't have but felt she was entitled to, if it were possible. She's very determined and intelligent and I don't think will be led into anything blindly. The Chaplain has since talked to me about it. Naturally I feel very happy about it but at the same time it's becoming quite embarrassing at times. He told me to suffer the embarrassment rather than keep even one soul out of the church.

So you see, the good Lord has already rewarded me a hundred fold for whatever sacrifice I have made in coming into this Army. Remember that always, no matter what might happen to me.

3 Sep 44—Letter to Martha

In appearance I've changed—I do have quite a few gray hairs in my head—never had them before. It isn't worry that has put them there, for

I don't worry. I blame it on a vitamin deficiency. The real change though I believe is my attitude and outlook. No, I'm not cynical or bitter like some are becoming, nor am I rebellious. I've learned to accept everything—no matter what, in a quiet way. Nothing can get me excited—fear—even when the alert sounds—which it doesn't very often—doesn't get the better of me. I know, and realize as never before that the good Lord is taking care of us—no one else, so it seems to me, can do the job.

PART III

Patriotism and Leadership

First Lt. Wallace Edward Zosel was born in Oregon on January 1, 1920, and joined the U.S. Army in 1939. He served with the 666th Engineers Topographical Company as a topographical engineer. The War Department had accepted and published his pamphlet on training procedures for armored divisions. He was commissioned an officer in 1942 and was sent to Northern Ireland in November 1943. First Lieutenant Zosel wrote the following letter from Northern Ireland while awaiting assignment to combat. It is addressed to his son, who was expected to be born in five months, and it was to be opened in the event of his death. At an unknown date he was sent to France, and there he was killed on August 16, 1944—only twelve days after his son's birth—while preparing for the Normandy invasion. First Lieutenant Zosel is buried at the American Military Cemetery in Normandy. His son, Roger Zosel O'Brien of Oregon, who is a member of the American World War II Orphans Network (AWON), says that his mother gave him the letter on the day of his high school graduation, when he was sixteen.

First Lieutenant Wallace Edward Zosel. Courtesy of Roger O'Brien.

March 13, 1944

A Letter To My Son:

Hello, Buck. I suppose you are wondering what kind of a man your father is. Since there is a chance that you might never see me, I thought I'd better write a few lines to you.

I have thought a great deal about you, with hope and pride in my heart, since your mother sent me the good news that you are on the way. It does seem rather strange for me to be writing you inasmuch as you are still an embryo lodged in your mother's beautiful body; but some day you will be a man, someone to carry on with the building of America.

What do I want of you? So many things that I doubt if I can think of them all now. But don't worry about it, if you try to be a good man, you will get along alright. My father before me wanted me to be a better man than he was, and I want you to be a better man than I am. You will inherit a good mentality, so I do not doubt that you will have plenty of natural intelligence; however, one thing I must caution you on: hard work is the key to a healthy, happy life. Always plug along and try to do each job that comes up as thoroughly and as well as you can, and you will get along alright.

When we, your mother and I, decided to have you, I wanted someone to carry on my name, my blood, so that my life would carry on in you. But it was your mother who bore the main burden, and she went through a lot of pain to bring you into the world because she loved me so much that she wanted me to be the father of her children. If you are anything like I am, you will probably raise a little hell and have some wild times when you approach manhood, but always limit yourself, keep clean and healthy, for the greatest treasure in life is to have the love of a really good woman. Your mother is the finest woman I have ever met, and by her true loyal love I have the strength to meet the harsher things in life and the desire to be as good a man as possible. If you are as lucky as I have been in the choice of a mate, you will be a very happy man.

I am grateful that my son can grow in the best country in the world, and, believe me, we who are overseas really know how wonderful America really is. True, we, as well as you, have seen many things about the United States that we would like to have changed, but that is what we hope to do—by gradual evolution keep constantly improving America as the home of the common man. That is perhaps our chief reason for fighting this war, the hope that afterwards we will have a greater country where everyone can live in the maximum prosperity and happiness. Millions of us over here are working, and fighting, and dying because we want America to be a nation of hope for mankind. And that is why I am trying to impress it on you with a few phrases that may seem trite but are really solid gold, for you of the future generation must realize our desires, the hopes that keep us always striving; for on you will rest the major responsibility of building America's golden age. Never let a few hard knocks shake your faith in your country. The history of America is unique in the history of all Time, for here for the first time in the tale of mankind's upward plodding, we find that the history of the nation is synonymous with the story of the emancipation of Man. Gradual progress is always being made, even though one cannot always see it, because everyone in America desires to have the lot of the common man and they strive for this end. Yes, I too have been kicked in the pants many times by vicious circumstances, but I have gained a lot in life, and I realize that all the good things I have, I possess because I am a part of the United States of America.

Son, I want you to develop your physical abilities, too. I want you to be able to hike, and play ball, and shoot with the best of them. But whatever you are proficient at, never try to impress other people ostentatiously of your abilities for they will see your good qualities and give you credit for it. You must learn a little gambling, but do not let the passion overcome you, quit when you have lost only a little. Another social duty is drinking; learn your capacity and then stop at that point. Always hold your liquor, never let it get the best of you! (Very important.)

As you know, I am a soldier. I am not going to tell you what line of endeavor you must choose, but, since I think we shall have some form of conscription after this war, I will devote a little space to the subject.

The first rule to remember is that military service is a privilege. Since each man has all the good things he possesses because the national government has supplied the protection and nucleus of the cooperative effort which is civilization, it is the duty of each citizen to give certain services to the state.

You will find that the greatest pleasure in army service is that spirit of comradeship that always is prevalent because so many people depend upon one another for their mutual comfort, and, in war, existence. The chief value of the military life, though, is the training in discipline. A man soon shows his true colors when he enters the army and must meet varying circumstances without any of the fellows around him. It is the ultimate democracy, everyone starts from the ground up, and advancement depends chiefly on the solid qualities of a man's character. You will learn the simple life, the hardships, the basic, real values, and it all goes to make a better man of one.

As for warfare, I don't know whether it is right or wrong, I just know that we have always had it, and, considering myself a professional soldier, I have always been interested in seeking to increase my efficiency and capacity to meet it. I do know that it is awfully hard, miserable work and that it brings great suffering and unhappiness to the people who fall victim to it. I hope that you never have to engage in a war. But it does mold a man, temper his character, give him a great appreciation of the things he has formerly taken for granted. I know for myself that when this is over I'll never want to be unkind to anyone again.

It hurts the women most. They sit at home not knowing what is happening to their loved ones, and they imagine all kinds of exaggerated horrors that really don't exist. I know your mother is worrying about me right now, and I wish I could reassure her and comfort her, but I can't. And every time a soldier is killed and buried, some woman's heart is buried there, too. No, son, war is not a good thing.

Well, Buck, there are still so many things I want to tell you, I could write a book, but you will only realize them after you have lived them yourself. Remember, my son, that I am proud of you and hopeful that you will be a fine man, much better than I am. But don't try too hard or worry about it, because when one has the stuff in him, he won't fail.

Your father,
Wallace E. Zosel

. . .

Lt. Robert Lee Shannon, Jr., was born in Danville, Kentucky on January 25, 1922. His father was killed in a railroad accident when he was three months old. His mother, Lillian Brasel Shannon, returned to her home in Morgan County, Tennessee, and lived there until remarrying in 1929. The family then moved to Rockwood, Tennessee, where they lived until 1943. Lieutenant Shannon joined the Naval Reserve in 1942 while attending Tennessee Technological University in Cookeville, Tennessee, and was commissioned ensign in the U.S. Navy in early 1944. He was promoted to lieutenant junior grade in 1945 after fourteen months in the South Pacific, serving at Guam and Iwo Jima as deck officer and navigator of the U.S.S. Canotia. *The* Canotia *departed Pearl Harbor in early February 1945, arriving at Eniwetok, where she reported for duty with the Fifth Fleet. She sailed to Iwo Jima as bitter action raged ashore. Lieutenant Shannon wrote the following letter to his mother, Lillian Wilson, in Tennessee, shortly after the Battle of Iwo Jima and while his wife Noroma was five months' pregnant with their first child. His daughter, Melinda Shannon Freels of Georgia, contributed it for her father. After the Japanese surrender, the* Canotia *cruised the small islands of the western Carolines, searching for American and Allied ex–prisoners of war or Japanese soldiers. In 1946, Lieutenant Shannon joined the Atomic Energy Commission, the predecessor to the Department of Energy. He held a naval reserve commission as lieutenant commander and was recalled by the navy in 1951. He remained on active duty until 1952, and during this time he was assigned to the Test Activities Branch of the Division of Military Application in the Atomic Energy Commission's Washington headquarters. For his weapons test work while in Washington, he received a special commendation by Gordon Dean, then chairman of the AEC. While in the naval reserve, he also served as the commanding officer of the Knoxville naval reserve. In 1959, he became the head of the Department of Energy's Technical Information Center in Oak Ridge, Tennessee. During the 1970s, he also served as the American liaison officer for the International Atomic Energy Agency. His daughter says he was respected as an internationally known energy information expert and a pioneer in technical information. He was a recipient of the AEC's Sustained Superior Performance Award and the Tennessee Technological University Distinguished Alumni Award. He was a member of the Rotary Club, a talented musician, and a gardener. At the time of his unexpected death on April 22, 1978, he had been with the federal government for more than thirty-two years.*

Lieutenant Robert Lee Shannon, Jr. Courtesy of Melinda Shannon Freels.

[Excerpt]

March 8, 1945
Guess Where

Dear Mom and Dad,

. . . Noroma seems to worry a lot about me. I try my best to keep her from worrying, but I suppose it's only natural that she should, but at any rate I'll tell you like I've told her so many times, I'll always be okay. It takes more than a few thousand yellow-bellied Japs to stop the United States Navy, and I know what I'm talking about.

I've seen such tremendous force and power released on them that it would make you shudder to think of it let alone witnessing it as I. How any nation could harbor even the faintest thought of waging war on us is beyond my power of comprehension. If they only knew of the might and will and above [all] the spirit of Americanism beforehand. They've finally found what it means and now they are all caught like so many filthy rats in a trap, lacking even the incentive to fight back, so our lot falls to only open up an extermination process and go about it like cutting wheat in a field.

You can never realize the gigantic and terrible force and power that we have at our disposal, enough to even bring down the stars from the sky. The only thing is that we have to hunt them and that takes time. Danger? A certain amount to be sure, enough to make it exciting and feel the tingle of the greatest game of them all. After all so many thousands are killed falling on a cake of soap, so our position is that of an elephant against a snake. All I hate is the fact that this time element is so grossly involved. Maybe I sound harsh and mechanical, but after all we are living as so many machines without soft grass and hills and dogwood blossoms without chocolate cake and martinis and yes, without the women we love. Maybe we have lost some of our civilized ways. But what is to be expected but barbarism after it becomes necessary to revert to our barbaric ways. As I have told Noroma so many times, this is only an interlude to life. But fundamentally you cannot call it an interlude. What is life but what death and suffering and exultation and victory doesn't reflect. Yes, this is an interlude, but who knows but what war tends to put an edge on our insights and to sharpen our wits and cause reflective thinking about the philosophy of the whole world and even the intricate planetesimal system. It even awakens that which lies dormant in the unborn child and maybe even in the dead. Even perhaps in my son who is to come into this world of war. There is endowed in him a certain quality of mind and thinking power that can think and arbitrate problems without the utter disintegration of whole races of people.

Patriotism? Well, yes, there is patriotism among us, not the synthetic kind that comes forth in the war mongers and profiteers—the kind that is amassed in the throats of people when our national ensign is unfurled, or like as many sheep, cheer at a passing parade—but rather the kind which lies deep and still in the hearts of our defenders. They know the meaning of utter weariness and deadness of fatigue and hunger and thirst and lying in a mud filled hole with dank, slimy mud slivering into their very skins. But primarily I say that they also know the patriotism if it is called that which lies deep inside is the burning flame of their reason. It is all so very foolishly simple. Ideals? You may call it ideals if you wish. Maybe some soldier is doing all this for the right of spending all his money on Saturday night on women and whiskey. Maybe another is doing it because he wants the right to walk down any street and look all mankind in the eye and say I am as good as you and I have the right to be a worker in the sewers or to be president.

Maybe these are extreme views but you can't escape the realness of it. But the whole thought lies in the fact that a man is a man for what he is not, what he does, and sitting in a quiet church on Sunday mornings fill some with idealism, others with humbleness. Well, so much for the philosopher's holiday. It never fails but I go off the deep end when I sit down at a typewriter. Maybe it's good that I can get rid of my thoughts on paper. I haven't anybody of sufficient intelligence to discuss them with. . . .

Well, I guess that about does it for tonight. So write me soon and I sure would like to get a letter from the Old Man. I'd like to know more about his new job.

Until the next time,
All my love,
Robert

• • •

Lt. Col. H. Paul Wolfe was born in Weir, Kansas, on January 5, 1910. He was the division judge advocate with the Third Armored Division, First Army, and participated in the Normandy, northern France, Ardennes, and central Germany battles, including the Battle of the Bulge. As the division judge advocate, he was responsible for advising the commanding general regarding rules of engagement, handling prisoners of war, relations with citizens, and managing land in areas the Army liberated. He coordinated all court martials, and as time permitted, he provided legal counsel to individual soldiers. The first letter is an excerpt from one that Lieutenant Colonel Wolfe wrote home to his children on the day he landed on Omaha Beach, in 1944; the second excerpt is from a letter written from Germany. Both were contributed by his daughter, Cynthia Wolfe of Arkansas. After the war, Lieutenant Wolfe practiced law and then held the office of circuit judge for twenty-nine years in his hometown of Fort Smith, Arkansas. He retired in 1974 and died in 1976.

Lieutenant Colonel H. Paul Wolfe during a training mission in England prior to the invasion of Normandy. Courtesy of Cynthia Wolfe.

[Excerpt]

. . . . You will find some sand and pebbles in this little box that is inside the big one. That sand and the pebbles are from what is called the "Omaha Beach," where many of our American soldiers landed on D Day. At that particular place where I got this the fighting was especially hard, and many of our fine soldiers were killed by the Germans. Our boys died for our country on those sands so that we could have peace and all come home again. I would keep that sand—some day there will be a great monument on that beach in honor of our soldiers, and people from all over will come back and see it and put flowers on the sands. We can be very proud of our soldiers. . . .

Bushels of love,
Daddy Pop

[Excerpt]

Somewhere in Germany
Sunday, 12 November

Dear Mother and Dad:
. . . . I suppose everyone is settled down now after the election. Honestly, I could almost say that we didn't even know there was one going on. Everybody is naturally interested in just one thing over here, the war. It's a grim business but I think we will all be much better citizens when we get back. We unquestionably have the best army in the world, and all of the folks back home who are carrying the load back there can really feel proud of the representation they are getting over here. If you could see the miserable conditions and horror under which our boys are living a few miles from here, you would cry for them but you would be awfully proud at the same time. And they're the best fighters in the world.

I hope you don't still have us mixed up with the Third Army—Patton's outfit. We are in the First Army—the cream of the crop, and you watch, the First Army is going to be the one that will break thro' and win the war. Just wait and see. And the Third Armored Division will be in front because we are, truthfully, the spearhead of the First Army. I'm sure proud to be with this outfit—and you just watch us go! . . .

Lots of love,
Paul

• • •

Lance Johnson of California contributed this letter written by his great-uncle, Karl Meyer, who was a member of the Nazi party and fought for Germany. His role was akin to that of the adjutant to the mayor. Karl Meyer was killed by shrapnel fire in Russia in 1943. The letter was translated by Ingrid Meyer and Lance Johnson.

Karl Meyer (left) with brother Theo. Courtesy of Lance C. Johnson.

France, July 15, 1940

My dear Mother!

Yesterday, on Sunday, I found myself with my company viewing the historical WWI battlefields of Verdun. We had seen the most famous, Fort Vaux and Douaumont, and stood deeply impressed in the gigantic cemetery of Heroes (Heldenfriedhof), when I heard from Ernst Benker the grim news of Theo's death. It came like lightning from a clear blue sky, and at first I could not grasp it: Theo, my dear brother and best comrade, is no more! Nothing can explain the following minutes of agony I felt, even though we soldiers are jaded about death, because too often do we have to see a good buddy take leave from his comrades; we are used to keeping a straight, emotionless face, even when it comes down to life or death. But now it is my brother who took a sudden leave and whom I will <u>never</u> shall see again.

I had to accept it as a twist of fate that I received the message of his death in this place of endless and constant reminders of death and deep mourning. In this place there was no room for a minimal, egotistical pain. I walked along the endless rows of graves, and while my eyes wandered over the names of the dead, the ones of the soldiers that died for the fatherland, I tried to gain control over my pain.

How must you feel, dear Mother? One of your five sons lives no more! He has, like us and so many others who live in this great and confusing time, given his life for Germany.

I cannot comfort you, because I myself lost too much. But the knowledge that everything has a deeper sense must be enough, must help to remove any lingering doubts. Maybe he died in an exuberant ride on his motorcycle, a happy feeling in his heart that only those who were part of the powerful victory over France could feel!?

I know that he was a passionate soldier who was caught up in this heroic endeavor, so different from the work that filled his life the last few years.

Karl Meyer. Courtesy of Lance C. Johnson.

May he sleep in peace now after a short, but rich and not uneventful, life, that always was guided by his straightforward, honest and faithful character.

Dear Mother, even though I am so far from the homeland, I share this deep sorrow with you.

Most sincerely,
Your loyal son,
Karl

. . .

Sgt. Charles H. Norris was born July 21, 1923, in New Castle, Pennsylvania. He joined the U.S. Army on November 30, 1942, and served with the U.S. Anti-Tank Company, 415th Infantry Regiment, 104th Division, First Army.

They trained until August 1944, went to France, and then went into combat with the First Canadian Army in Holland before their division went with the First American Army into Germany, where they fought until they met the Russians. This letter was written from Eschweiler, Germany, when Sergeant Norris was in the battalion reserve in the middle of the Siegfried lines, to Mr. and Mrs. McConnell, the parents of Jean and Fred McConnell. Fred, a long-time school friend, was a member of the Air Force and now lives next door to Sergeant Norris. Sergeant Norris dated Jean and during the war wrote hundreds of letters to her and several to her parents, which she recently returned to him. Sergeant Norris was discharged in November 1945 and went back to work for the Pennsylvania Power Company a few days after returning home. He was recalled to duty in 1950 and spent seven months in Korea. He again returned to the United States to work for the Pennsylvania Power Company and retired after forty-five years. He still lives in Pennsylvania.

Sergeant Charles Norris standing next to one-and-a-half-ton Dodge Prime-Mover used to tow their 57-mm anti-tank gun. Courtesy of Charles Norris.

Germany
Nov. 22, 1944

Dear Mr. and Mrs. McConnell,

I am living in a fine house today and these people are far better off than most people as they use a better grade of stationery than most people.

I received your letter a few days ago but I am too busy most of the time to answer any letters.

I'm still having a swell time most of the time but every once in awhile I get hell scared out of me. There still are a few German soldiers left in Germany.

I fought in Belgium and Holland and the fighting up there was a pushover but these Germans fight better in their backyard. And please don't let anyone talk you into the idea that the war is over. People should write to the Germans and tell them that the war will be over in a few months.

Up in Holland I was getting the hell shelled out of me one day and just then a flight of our army bombers flew over and I was never so glad to see the Air Corps in my life and what do you think those bastards dropped—leaflets, telling the Germans to surrender. I sat in my foxhole for one hour and called the Air Corps and your son everything on earth. I was never so mad in my life.

Something funny like that happens every day and it will take months to tell you all about this war when I get home.

We sit around and laugh till we get sick sometimes and at the same time we are being shelled by the enemy. The American soldier will have a good time no matter where he goes.

We cook most of our own meals and it is my turn to cook supper. I will open up ten cans of C rations and heat them up on the stove and serve them on good china. The German civilians have evacuated this town and we are using their houses and good china.

Love,

Chuck

• • •

Pfc. Fielding D. Tucker served in the U.S. Army in the European theater of operations. He wrote letters home to Mississippi, including this one to a friend with whom he had worked. Private First Class Tucker now lives in Georgia.

Private First Class Fielding D. Tucker. Courtesy of Fielding D. Tucker.

Germany
May 16, 1945

Dear VBR,

Thought I would drop you a few lines to let you know I am still OKAY. You know, I feel kind of lucky seeing fifteen months of combat over here without getting a scratch. Yet, I've seen the times I wouldn't give a penny for my life.

Last February I came over here with fifty-nine men; there are only four of us left. One of these boys is a swell friend of mine, Daniel Tubb.

It happened the morning after the night we moved up to relieve another outfit. Two squads of our platoon dug in. The other remained at the house where we set up our CP to run patrols. It was my squad that ran the patrol; Tubb's squad dug in with the other in the grape vineyards.

About a thousand yards away there was a town burning from shell fire. We patrolled so close to the town that we could see the time on the town clock. Ammunition was exploding. We could smell the livestock burning. We knew there were Germans in the town, because they were firing their machine guns every few minutes.

Well, when we returned to the company with the information, we were told to get a little rest, because my squad was to go out and relieve Tubb's squad the next morning; but I was to leave for rest camp at daylight.

About three hours later, gunfire awoke me, I went to the window and saw Germans running around. We tried to call by phone to the boys dug in, but the wires were cut, even the ones back to the battalion CP. So, the only thing for us to do was to post ourselves at the doors and windows. I stood by the kitchen door.

Through the windows at a distance I saw three Americans being stripped of their fighting equipment. One of these boys was Tubb. About the same time a man came to the door with a can of gas that he had taken from our antitank truck parked at the front of the house. His intentions, or rather orders, were to burn us out. We saw each other at the same time; I fired my Thompson not wanting to hit him but he was there.

When battalion got wise to what was happening they sent reinforcements with a tank up to help us and did a swell job of doing it. Our two squads were captured. The Germans lost about fifty men.

The German that came into the kitchen door was just about to be searched for papers. I touched him and he looked up to me and said: "Kamerad all is kaput."

I saw that he was hit in the knees of both legs.

Enclosed you will find a letter sent to me from Tubb's mother. He's free now, I know.

Well, VBR, I must close this note now as there are no lights in my room. Hope to see you soon.

Fielding

At the present time I am in a small town near Munich.

· · ·

Pvt. Ian McNeur served as a member of the Second New Zealand Expeditionary Force, Second New Zealand Division, Fifth New Zealand Infantry Brigade, Twenty-third Battalion Signals Platoon, D Company. He saw active duty in the Italian campaign prior to being wounded at Cassino on April 4, 1944, as he relates in the following poem entitled "Last Night," which was contributed by his son, George McNeur of Christchurch, New Zealand. "Last Night" is part of the World War II collection in the New Zealand Army Museum in Waiouru, New Zealand, and on Ian McNeur's website http://kiwisoldier.4mg.com.

LAST NIGHT

Tonight's the night the word runs
Into the line once more;
Maleish! The game's a grim one,
But such is life in war.

Private Ian McNeur in Cairo, Egypt, February 7, 1943. Courtesy of George McNeur.

Ammo and iron rations,
The wireless, that's enough.
Just feel the weight, your back will break
Carrying all that stuff.
But still, a man might need it
If Jerry cuts up rough.

Jolting through starry blackness
Smoke tips point the dark.
Cobbers all and merry
As on a boyish lark.
Stillness! "OK, you've had it."

From here on boys, it's feet.
Gear on, we hit the roadway
The moonlit night to greet.
Ahead the grim Cassino
Where Hell and soldier meet.

Heft the pack, tommy alert,
Finger the ready grenade,
Along the track who knows what waits.
Life is of seconds made.
Down the track, we're in it now,
Into the stinking smoke.
He's shelling too, duck, duck me lad
That one's much too close.
Faster boss, this place is hot.
Down! Up and on again.
OK? No—duck, he's on to us;
I'll get ducks on the brain.
Another close, a big 'un too,
Came whistling like a train.
Turn left, that building there,
A hundred yards to go.

What—?uuh!—you've had it lad
You're hit. Still living though.
Now what is wrong? The head's OK
Brain clear as a bell.
My eye! The thing can't see
May work—time yet will tell.
But wait, it's just some blood.
It can see fairly well.

Left hand is crook, two fingers bust.
That shrap did quite a job.
The groin is numb, right leg still works.
Must crawl and join the mob.
But first a prayer, it's courage lad
You'll need before the dawn.

And thanks be, you're still alive
And still in working form.
Thus in the very shade of death
The gates of Hell are torn.
Now pull that strap across your head.
That buckle sure is tight.
Gear off and now the thing's to crawl,
Right arm, both legs, you're right.
Another foot and then one more,
And now to cross this hole.
This iron bar—must go round it.
That mortar made you roll.
And now the building to get through
A doorway or a hole.

They're cutting the gloves your mother made
To get at the wounded mit.
Your trousers too and the tunic now—
They were a lovely fit.
Your clothes are off except the shirt
And your wallets are there me lad.
Your wounds are dressed, but boy, you're weak,
Still, they don't feel bad.
The stretcher's here, now to the jeep,
And you've started home me lad.

. . .

Lt. Walter Best served in the German Wehrmacht in an antitank unit Panzer-Jaeger-Abteilung 295. His nephew, Harald Thomas of Pulheim, Germany, who translated and contributed his uncle's letters, says, "Being fascinated by driving cars, Walter Best soon became a member of the Nationalsozialistisches Kraftfahrer-Korps (NSKK), a party organization that gave young men the opportunity to qualify for a driver's license and to drive cars belonging to this organization. Moreover, the NSKK would teach them Nazi ideology. Somehow Walter Best was infected by this ideology, too, and, after some time, leading the local NSKK organization at Wiesbaden became his chief occupation. His rank in this organization was 'Standartenführer,' which was then equal to the military rank of a colonel." He also moved with his wife, Ria, to a neighboring village, where they lived next door to the "Reichsjugendfuehrer" (Leader of the National Youth) Baldur von Schirach and became acquainted with well-known Nazi leaders. After the German invasion of Poland and the onset of World War II, Walter Best volunteered as a regular soldier of the German army although his rank in the Nazi hierarchy would have made it easy for him to stay at home. He advanced through the ranks as a corporal, sergeant, and second lieutenant. From autumn 1940 to spring 1941 he served with the German occupation forces in Abbéville, France, until his unit was transferred to occupied Poland. When Germany invaded Russia in 1941, Walter Best served as a platoon leader in an antitank unit (Panzer-Jaeger-Abteilung 295). He was awarded several medals, such as the Eisernes Kreuz (Iron Cross) second and first class. After his death he was awarded the Verwundetenabzeichen (medal for wounded soldiers) and the medal for the Russian winter campaign, often called the "frozen meat medal." Walter Best's last letter is dated January 23. The following day he was mortally injured by a gunshot in his chest during a Russian attack. He was buried in the village of Orechowatka in Russia.

[Excerpt]

January 8, 1942

My dear little Ria,

This is a sweet day, for your letters containing pudding and sugar arrived, together with a journal and your letter written Dec. 18. I'd like Private Reh to cook a pudding, but unfortunately it is too late now. Reh is my new attendant, and he is very useful. He cooks well, but there is not much left to cook. But I already wrote you that we will not starve. Tomorrow we will search for different things to eat. I hope we will get a hog again.

For the next two days I will not be able to write you. We go back in. . . . The Russians don't attack any longer. So I can care about the partisan job more intensively.

In general the whole story makes more sense again, here. I could not tell you more about our desperate situation during the last weeks. Relatively weak German forces had fought their way on good roads along the Sea to Rostow. Then bad weather came and all the mud. So we could not reach our destination. Our front line looked like a huge bend. When the first frost came, the Russians put so much pressure on Rostow, that this bend had to be withdrawn. From our sector all forces were moved to the South, and the result was we had to defend an extremely large sector. You can compare it to the distance between Armsheim and Wiesbaden (60 km). Normally a regular division has to defend a front line up to 9 km. But since there were many casualties, our companies are no longer complete. Can you imagine this narrow line of defence, repelling several Russian divisions for weeks? But now things look much better. And our Ju-88 (diving bombers) are on duty again since yesterday. You can imagine that I was a little bit nervous during the last time. But now everything is better and the cold has abated, too.

Your brother, Willi, was lucky with his wounding. I suppose he will be with you on furlough, soon. Bad luck is good luck! Best regards to him, if you see him at home!

What do I think of our strategic position? I wrote you about this several times. Still I think that Turkey should be the main object of our diplomatic efforts. If we could reach the Caucasian oil wells from Turkey, the decision in this war would be given. Without any doubt the Japanese have excellent soldiers and Roosevelt probably does not like the results of his naval war. Nevertheless the final decision will be given here in the East. When Russia is finished off, Britain and America may do whatever they want. Our economic and military resources and our basis of nutrition will be much more promising then. Continuing the war would be madness for both Britain and America. In this case Britain will give up soon. But even a latent state of war, which is thinkable, could be maintained to the end with a small part of our armed forces only. The question remains: What is the situation in the East?

In the beginning of the campaign the Russians outnumbered us in men and material equipment. Partly they had better weapons than we had. There is something you should not ignore: The Russian soldier is extremely stubborn. His life deems him as worthless as a dog's life. And that's the way he dies, like a dog. He is unable to judge that the situation in general is hopeless. As long as he is pushed forward or is forced to defend himself, he will shoot. But when the pressure stops, because the commissars were killed or deserted, then he will desert or surrender.

You cannot expect the mass of Russian soldiers to kill their commissars. They are no longer capable of doing this. It is hard to tell how 23 years of Soviet regime changed people here. You cannot even compare them to an animal, for there are even dogs that bite their master's whip. The Russians reject Stalin and the whole Soviet system as much as the mouse rejects the cat. This comparison hits the nail on the head.

I had to explain this so that you understand my evaluation of the situation. As long as Stalin pushes on his commissars and these commissars push on the soldiers the war will go on. It will be over when there are no more Russian soldiers or if Stalin gives up. It does not matter if Stalin is only an instrument or if he is the master. Anyway he and his wire-pullers are not fighting for Russia but for the Communist world revolution. This is the reason why they do not act in favor of Russia or the Russians. They will take every chance to gain their ends, and this last chance is the last Russian soldier. There is no hope of a revolution by the people to remove Stalin. The only chance might be one of Stalin's confidants, who likes Russia and the Russians more than the Communist world revolution. I wonder if there is such a person or even more of them. Hitler and Ribbentrop will know better. But there is only a little hope. So, all that is left is the last Russian soldier.

Last year the Russians lost many men and a lot of their equipment; moreover, they lost their best troops and most of their best weapons. Even by mobilizing new armies they will not be able to achieve their former strength again. And they cannot provide them with the same equipment the now defeated armies had. You can see this even without looking at maps showing Russia's industrial centers. For I believe that the Russians built up armament factories in the Urals and in Siberia. Anyway they lost most of their war factories, and they will not be able to manufacture the same amount of goods within 5 months of war, with only a few factories left, that they produced in 1940–41 in 18 months in peace—even with America's support.

What you can see right now are Russian soldiers attacking us without guns. Without any doubt the Russians have well-equipped armies, too, but these are only minor parts, the last reserves gathered from Siberia and the Caucasus.

Next spring the Russians will be able to set armed forces against us, which—in the very best case—are equal to ours in numbers and materiel equipment. Regarding all these aspects, the war here in Russia still might last six months. And surely there is no optimism at all in this calculation.

There is one thing you must not forget: All the small countries like Hungary, Bulgaria, Finland, etc. could dispatch only a few soldiers, since they do not have enough equipment. This is the main problem with Italy, too. We will use our huge Russian booty to equip the armies of these countries. Even our soldiers will use Russian weapons. In spring things will look different, as our own industry will produce at its maximum limit.

The most difficult time is now defending the front line. For the Russians can concentrate their forces at will. But now they can no longer hide their troops, so we can counter their movements. So e.g. we knew about the last assaults the Russians made before. Anyway Stalin's hope he put in the Russian winter will not come true, and in spring his war will be lost for him.

My darling, I gave you a very detailed description of the situation. Now I must go to sleep, for I have to rise early in the morning.

Sleep well, my darling. I wish this letter were with you as fast as my thoughts or—even better—that I were with you as fast as my thoughts! But then I would be always with you and I wouldn't have to travel.

Best wishes and many kisses,

your Walter

* * *

The following letters were written by 1st Lt. Clarence Eugene ("Bud") Zieske, who was killed in action on August 12, 1944, in Rosiers, France. First Lieutenant Zieske served with the Eighth Army Air Force, 361st Fighter Group, 374th Fighter Squadron. The letters were written to his wife, Jeanne. First Lieutenant Zieske's brother, 1st Lt. Vernon Lloyd ("Zeke") Zieske, was killed in action on January 26, 1945, in Belgium. He served with the Ninth Army Air Force, 36th Fighter Group, 23rd Fighter Squadron. The brothers are buried beside each other in Arlington National Cemetery, Washington, D.C. The letters were contributed by Bud's son and Zeke's nephew, Joseph Mack Zieske Ormond of California.

First Lieutenant Clarence Eugene Zieske. Courtesy of Joseph Ormond.

June 25, 1944
England

Dearest Jeanne,

Well here we are with another week gone by. This week sure seems to have gone pretty fast. I guess that is because we have been pretty busy.

I gather from your letters that my mail has been taking its good old time at reaching the States. Just you wait, you will probably get several in a bunch. I think they have been holding everything over here because of the big excitement. By the time this reaches you they will have no doubt relaxed a little and you will receive the letters soon after they are written. I have been wondering why you had never mentioned in your previous letters that you had received my cable. It was only supposed to take about a day or so but it looks like it took more than a week.

We have had quite a dreary day today with nothing doing at all so we played bridge most of the time. I was going to see the picture tonight but the line up was too long there to wait so I'll see it tomorrow. It is "North Star." I hear it is supposed to be a good show. I saw "Tender Comrade" a couple nights back. That to me was not too good. Remember the big argument we had the night after you had seen it. I guess that was one reason why I didn't like the show. I went into see it with a critical eye and an unpleasant memory of what it had brought about a few weeks back.

And now I shall make a few requests that we keep you busy for a little while at least. Things which are scarce over here seem to be those things I like. Mainly cookies and candy bars are what I really go for in a big way. So if you can gather together some of these, send them my way. You should be able to buy some candy bars at Fort Hayes. I think with that pass of yours you should not have trouble shopping there at the commissary. I'm also having a bit of a time with the means of lighting my cigarettes so if you can find a lighter anywhere in town send that along also. You will have to take this letter to the post office when you send the package to show that I requested a package sent over here. I believe there is a restriction to the size of the package but it can be quite large I believe. Not large enough for you to get into though. Isn't that our tough luck. You probably could have made it a little while back but it would cramp you a little too much at present.

What do you mean in your letter by saying that you and flying are so much different with me? Don't you know that where both of you are concerned it is like being up in the clouds and away from all the rest of the world? When I'm with you I'm floating on air likewise when I'm flying. Of course there is a difference but you know what I mean. I will be truthful though and tell that when I'm flying I don't have time to miss you. I'm too concentrated on seeing that everyone else misses me. So far so good and all I suffer is a sore bottom from sitting too long in one spot and on one spot.

Glad to hear that you and the young one are coming along alright. I do hope you get over those sick spells soon. As the doctor says they are no good. Listen to me talking like an old midwife or something.

Well this is about all for now so I'll close. God bless you and the baby. Keep safe and well.

With all my love,
Bud

Saturday afternoon
[August 5, 1944]

Darling Jeanne,

Well I had better get back at this writing before it goes on too long. We have been quite busy around here lately. I've been flying long hours every day and you would not believe it but I'm getting to the point where I would just like to stand on the ground for a while. Boy I never knew my backside could get so sore from flying. Try sitting in a chair and being strapped in for six hours and see how sore you get. Of course you got more padding than I have so you probably will only be half as sore as I get. I now have as much time over here in one month of flying than I got in three months at Pinellas.

Little Smith finally showed up over here. Boy did we pass those fellows up. Of course they had a whole month at Tallahassee that we didn't get. Let me tell you, sweetheart, that is something I would really go for right now. You know, Honey, I not only count the days when I shall receive a letter from you but also count the day when I shall be back again with you. I love you so much it really hurts me to think about it.

First Lieutenant Vernon Lloyd Zieske. Courtesy of Joseph Ormond.

Of all the girls in this wide world there is only one that I want to be with and that is you and only you. Darling, I think of you all through the day and dream of being with you all during the night. I guess about the most wonderful thing that ever happened to me was when I came on to you. I know I'm not the real romantic type of a husband but I do my best to show how dearly I love you. If you miss me at all you can surely count on me missing you just twice as much. Someday you and I and our family shall all be together again and we will again have a wonderful time. My letters are not very newsy but I write them just to keep reminding you how much I love you and miss you. Someday I shall be able to tell you all about what I'm doing. I must close now as more has come up

Your Ever Loving,
Bud

I love you, Sweetheart, very much

The following letter was postmarked August 13, 1944, and was the last letter that Jeanne received.

11 Aug 1944

Darling Jeanne,

Received two letters from you today, both of them sent on the third of the month. You can see that mail is starting to arrive now in little or no time. Of course there will probably be some back mail coming through. There must be some cause you mention things which you wrote in other letters but from their nature I can tell I haven't received the previous letters.

There are two or three things I wish you would put me straight on. To start off with did you ever receive the fifty dollar check I sent home? Next did you ever receive the little bracelet made out of English coins? And last of all did you receive my letter about sending over that envelope that I had previously sent home from New York?

Now that that is over with we shall dispense with such questions. I thought the pictures you sent over were very nice. I see what you mean by your broadside view. You must be putting on a little weight ha!

I can let loose on a few questions you probably have been wondering concerning what I'm doing over here. I think I've already told you I was flying Mustangs and I guess you know how well I like that airplane. Dad asked me in his note enclosed in your letter as to what Air Force I was in. Well I'm in the illustrious Eighth Air Force from which hails all the Aces of this theater of war. I guess you didn't get what I was trying to explain when I mentioned getting a little extra education around here. Point it out to Dad, maybe he can figure it out. I'm enclosing a picture taken of me in the cockpit of my airplane. Of course all you can see is me but you wouldn't want to look at an airplane anyhow.

I received your packages of candy and cookies. The cookies were a little the worse for wear and crushed but I salvaged the crumbs and they were very good.

Well this is all for now. I must get some sleep. Keep well and safe. I love you very much, Darling, and miss you too much.

Your loving,
Bud

Officers Club
Bradley Field
Connecticut
3 July 1944

Dear Bud,

Today, I received your V-Mail letter. Also I received a letter from mother saying they and Jeannie had heard from you. I hope you can continue to keep the folks and Jeannie informed as to your well-being.

Perhaps you'd be interested in knowing my tragic metamorphosis in the past fateful month of June; I have given up my wonderful position as a flight commander and potential captain to accept a dubious honor of becoming a "trainee" in the 1st Air Force. I have become a part of the recently graduated class of 44-D. Believe me, it is quite a blow to take some of this nonsense. But of course you know what I'm talking about. I left Naples on the 1st of June and haven't flown since. There are rumors (as there always are) that we are ready to start now—this is some time next week.

From what I have seen of this base and this Air Force (1st), it is difficult for me to see how anything is accomplished. They are completely swamped with regulations—base regulations, 1st Fighter Command regulations, 1st Air Force regulations.

Under Col. T——— at Naples, we found we could get along quite well with existing regulations of the Army Air Force and the A.R.'s

However, those days are gone forever and I imagine I'll be forever trying to accustom myself to anything else.

I must only write one page in order to stay under the limit for airmail overseas, so this is it. Write often, Bud, perhaps I may see you sometime in October or November.

Your brother,

Vernon

Good flying

. . .

The following letter was written the day Vernon's younger brother, Bud, was killed in action.

Officers Club
Bradley Field
Connecticut
12 Aug 1944

Dear Bud,

Your latest letter came yesterday and I was very glad to hear you are enjoying yourself. Many congratulations on finishing your ten "trips." I was also happy to hear that you know how to wreck a ship without killing yourself. Don't let that little landing accident bother you.

Here in the First Air Force, we have access to all the S-2 poop of the VIII Fighter Command, and I have been watching with emphasized interest the reviews of the 361st Fighter Group. It is quite an organization. I am always hoping to see your name under the "claims" column.

Well, life here in the states is very much the same as always. My training here is slowly coming into its own. I transferred into Air Force on the 6th of June and today I have a total of 20 hours, 5 in A-24 and 15 in a P-47. The flying here is not all dull and tiresome. The instructors are fine fellows, most of them ex-combat men. My flight leader flew a P-38 against the Japs to the tune of nine kills.

The weather here in Connecticut is lousy. Haze, smoke, low ceilings all help keep one's flying at a minimum. It is seldom the visibility ever gets over 2 miles.

By degree, I am learning to like the P-47. It is fondly referred to on this base as "the monster." I guess with the super gasoline of the combat theaters and the later models that they are using over there, they do have a rather impressive record.

I surely am glad you like your airplane. It is a real honey, I'm sure. I have a definite affinity for in-line engines.

Well, here is the second page already and I'm still going strong. I'm writing this in my room. It is 10:00 and I have to be at the line at 12:15 usually, if our flight flies in the afternoon, as today. We are all in the gym knocking ourselves out, but today is Saturday, there is no class in calisthenics. We've already finished our four weeks of ground school and we will have none of that until we transfer to the advanced RTU. You see, the system here is different from that at Pinellas. We get half our time here and half at another base. Why? Your guess is as good as mine.

There is no news of any special magnitude from home. Everyone is happy and healthy. Mother and Jackie had food poisoning a few weeks ago but all is well now. Dad's garden, as usual, is the best in the neighborhood. And he is working hard on the railroad. I hope to get a leave next month. The policy here is not too sharp along granted leaves but I am still hoping.

From the looks of things as we get them via newspapers, radio and *Time*, I don't imagine you fellows over there are going to need my helping efforts, so I imagine I'll be spending Christmas on a square acre in the middle of the broad Pacific.

Good Hunting. Write.
Vernon.

PART IV

Life in the Military

First Lt. Jennis ("Jack") Strickland served as a B-24 bomber pilot with the U.S. 445th Bomber Group stationed in England. On March 24, 1945, he was piloting the deputy lead plane for the Eighth Air Force, Second Air Division, raid on Wesel, Germany—Operation Varsity, the crossing of the Rhine—when his plane was shot down and he was killed. His wife, Kitty Strikland Shore of Maryland, and her son, Jack Strickland, Jr., contributed the following letter written by First Lieutenant Strickland to his crew before they left for England in 1944. According to Kitty, his second letter was written after a raid on Osnabruck, Germany, and the target on the next two raids, on the fourteenth and seventeenth, was Köln, Germany. First Lieutenant Strickland's letters can be found in Red Roses and Silver Wings *by Kitty Strickland Shore, published by AAM Press, P.O. Box 15175, Chevy Chase, Maryland 20825. For more information, please consult their web site at www.aampress.com.*

First Lieutenant Jack Strickland (standing on far right) with his original crew beside a B-24 just before they left for England. Courtesy of Kitty M. Shore.

Well, you guys,

Looks like the time is just around the corner when we're going to cease being just a crew in training.

Guess you all are just as fed up as I am with training, day in, day out. We've all done our share of griping in the army and we will probably do a lot more before it's over. Let's get one thing straight now, though. Tomorrow we're going to be dodging the same bullets, eating the same food, getting the same amount of sleep when we can. Tomorrow we cease being individuals. We will be a team in the army, fighting the same fight, griping the same gripes and looking forward to getting home with the same feeling of being fed up with all this. One thing stands out, though; we're still in the army with an assigned job to be done. That particular job calls for all-out cooperation between each and every one of us. Tomorrow those who still have the idea of getting through this thing the easiest possible way, well, those that STILL have that idea are letting the rest down. Not only are you putting a harder job on someone else's shoulders—you're selling them down the river. Worse even than showing up with a solid yellow streak down your back. Believe me, brother, you're going to be treated as such if that's the case.

Lately there's been quite a lot of bitching (you're in the army, now). First, it's flying too much—secondly, it's getting up too early and lately it's paying too much attention to how much work the other guy is doing and forgetting your own.

Most of us have already buckled down, gotten the harness as comfortable as possible and started the load rolling toward the other end. The road is long, maybe around the world—one thing is certain, though—at the end is home—bright and shining.

To those guys on this crew who still think they're in the army just because it's the only place to wait out the war—I've got something special to say.

Every one of us has had a certain amount of specialized training, some have worked at it, learned it—and possibly have done even better at it than was expected of them. Those are the ones that realize there's a war going on and that someone's going to get hurt. They're the ones that have done their best all the way and intend doing the same the rest of the way. To their comrades in arms, they are insurance—not only life insurance but insurance that this thing will be ended as soon as they have dragged the load home—right up to the front door.

The others are parasites, hanging on—dragged through by others. They're the ones who have time to really bitch in earnest. They are the ones who are going to regret it the rest of their lives. Their time is a little more limited than the rest—but on a crew like this, they are putting a time limit on the other guys.

Before I finish this little "sermon" there is one more subject I would like to cover: leaves and furloughs. Naturally all of us expect a little time off now and then. For awhile it looked as if we might get home and see the folks before we were called to do the job we have been training for. Now that the time is close at hand, maybe we won't get that chance. You are a man now and above all else you're supposed to be soldiers. Starting right now, let's be just that. Being [of] above average intelligence, we should realize it's up to us to do our duty as such and do it to the best of our ability. That way we will get this thing over much quicker and much easier.

Maybe some of us haven't stopped to think what we're fighting for. At any rate there are still a few left in the crew that show signs of selfish ideas about how the war is to be won. The idea that the other guys have done a pretty good job up until now, so why not let them finish it—is out. They will find in a very short while that they're OUT, too, so far as the rest are concerned.

Think it over, soldier, or else you'll be calling me chicken. From now on I'm in deadly earnest. I expect the same of each and every one of you.

Let's hope that when we drop the harness and look around us at the guys that were in step beside us, we'll have the satisfaction of a job well done. You'll know that you won't have to lie the rest of your lives when you tell your children how we won the war.

Lt. J. M. Strickland
(Pilot)

[Excerpt]

Oct. 12, 1944

Dear Miss,

'Bout time you came over and chased this melancholy feeling away, don't you think? These nights that we have to walk over to the latrine to shave—well, the stars and clouds and the fading moon, you can guess who I'm thinking of. Romantic walk, ain't it?

Today was the first day of firsts in about every way you can think of.

Your first letter since the States and it was written on a young man's first birthday. Here's hoping it's the beginning of continuous mail, however it's probably a far-fetched hope—for awhile anyway.

Yesterday I had one of those peculiar army experiences—with a smile thrown in. During chow—it's more or less cafeteria style—except the choice—well I'm walking along holding out my plate. The K.P.s behind the counter put a slurp of something here, a slurp of something there, then slurp a big gob of slush over the whole thing which has run together anyway. Comes dessert—home canned sour cherries—not bad. Then I glance up. My eyes bulge a bit and a big burst of laughter wells up, get red in my face—finally bust out. Since I'm still holding out my plate, the K.P. says, "More?"

"No." Since my mustache is rank enough to mow off now, he don't recognize me. (Mowing it soon as I get one snapshot.) "Don't you recognize me?"

"No, SIR, I mean, Yes, SIR."

"I'm Strickland."

"Well, I'll be a #!:**and!;sl. What in hell are you doing here, Jack?" So we gab, hold up the line, slap each other on the back. Every time I look at the guy I bust out all over again. You know him, too. Nice looking, chunky, blond, usually a crew cut. No? Well, too bad so I'll change the subject.

Wrote Harold and Harp yesterday. Have hopes of an answer within two weeks.

Today we ran the gamut, so far as emotions are concerned. Turned on the Bomb run—mind blank—no thoughts—then realize I'm humming way back in my mind, "I love coffee, I love tea, etc." Why'n hell, I don't know. Must have been the Ink Spots I heard on a program a while ago. All this passes through my mind, then, like a dream, thoughts race, thick and fast. Pull it in closer (the formation). Steady, now. Hell's sort of concentrated up ahead. Here we go. Guess it'll be concentrated down below now. Shame to wreck all those things down below. Hope the people get to safety. (Am I soft!) There it goes—just as mean and concentrated a dose of medicine as man can make—almost. Well guess it will bring the end at least two days closer and slow up the opposition against Harold and Harp and all those guys. By this time we're getting out—fast—running, if you please. WUMP—a slight jar and we're clear. Let's head for home now—pretty chilly up here, right foot numb. Funny how the pilots sweat—wet sweat—and their feet freeze. So, turn up the electric suit—adjust the connection and gradually your feet burn a little, thaw out, feel nice and comfortable. Little shack, here we come. That bunk's going to feel good. Wish I didn't have on so darn much equipment—or else the relief tube were closer—oh well, grin and bear it—hope you can, anyway. Surprise, you didn't—I mean, you DID. Back on the ground—now for relief. Everyone chattering at once. "Hey, Skipper, did you see so and so?" (conceited, aren't I?) and now I find if I stand still my knees shake—somewhat like they do under the dinner table, except I'm standing up. Wow! Must be fatigue, eh, what?

Here we are at operations and I get a warm feeling. There's the blond guy, the aircraft mechanic on KP. The corporal's waiting—or did he just happen to be here? Funny, his squadron's operations are elsewhere. Then again, maybe I'm conceited. Makes me feel good anyhow—but how did he know I was up? We grin, swap cracks and move on. There's a lot to do yet before we eat and turn in for a long nap. The guy, in case you're interested, knows you—and I think you'll remember him. His name? Burns!—My former boss at the Goodrick Economy Store—surprised?

... Be seeing you, Miss. Lots of love—full, rich—not automatic, lean—and you can quote me.

Jack

• • •

First Lt. Lawson Corley signed up for pilot training the day after the bombing of Pearl Harbor and was a bombardier in the 705th Bomber Squadron,

Eighth Air Force, in 1944 when his plane was shot down over Belgium and he was taken as a prisoner of war by the Germans. He served eleven months in the Nazi prison camps known as the Sweatbox, Dulag Luft, Stalag Luft III (Sagan), Stalag XIII-D (Nurnburg), and Stalag VII-O (Moosburg). He survived two death marches. Then, in April 1945, Patton's Third Army liberated him and his fellow prisoners. He has vivid memories of a pillar of smoke on the horizon rising from a nearby concentration camp called Dachau. First Lieutenant Corley's letter was written in April 1943 to his then-fiancée and later wife, Florence. At the time, he was attending bombardier training school at Victorville Air Force Base—now Edwards Air Force Base. First Lieutenant Corley runs the Lawson Corley Museum of Arrowheads, Indian Artifacts, and War Memorabilia in Birmingham, Alabama, and is a popular speaker about World War II and active in veterans' affairs.

Say, I've been so terribly busy the last two weeks that I haven't had the time to write you much about the little excitement we have had here.

On Sunday night (April 25) I was on guard duty and as I looked into the moonlight sky I saw searchlights comb [the sky] and many P-38 Interceptors took-off only two blocks away!! The alarm was sounded so we guards hurried thousands of Cadets to their barracks where they got their gas masks then they were marched to disbursal spots off the Post. Everyone but we guards was evacuated so it was very lonely in the total darkness alone! Soon the search lights spotted the unidentified plane and I heard anti-aircraft fire! The "enemy" then gave the proper signal so it was permitted to land. The "all-clear" was sweet music to my ears!

One day last week we were told to carry our gas masks until the raid. We were just going to noon chow when an Army plane flew over just ten feet from the ground and dropped bombs of gas! We had to get into our masks and leave them on for over 30 minutes!

Last Monday I had a pleasant time doing K.P. for seventeen continuous hours!! On Tuesday I was in charge of 193 of us that went to the firing range down on the beach. I made top scores with the aerial and Thompson machine guns and rang the bull's eye with the rifle and .45 cal. pistol! We got to go swimming in the blue Pacific so I added to the tan I'm acquiring here in sunny California.

Today we marched to a field where we had to run into clouds of poisonous gases, take a sniff, detect what it was, then run to safety! We were also shown how the new Air Corps fire bomb will burn through water and steel!

I am a Flight Sergeant now (Cadet Captain in two weeks), so I bunk down here with the other officers, near the Orderly Room, so I get to peck on this typewriter a little now and then.

• • •

Sgt. Clifford Tompkins served with Company F, Twenty-sixth Infantry, before he was killed in action on June 12, 1944. Sergeant Tompkins wrote the following letters to one of his brothers, Reuben Tompkins of Westerlo, New York. In his letter, Clifford and Reuben are sons of Maude (Luther) and Leonard Daniel Tompkins. The other four siblings are Harry, Earl, Clinton, and Bessie. These letters were contributed by Sergeant Tompkins's niece, Marie Hardin of New York.

12:30 Noon
Fort Benning
May 29, 42

Dear Brother,

Received your letter yesterday. Was glad to hear from you + that you are all well. I guess your letter got delayed a little on account of its going down to Fla. + then coming back here at Fort Benning.

We are camped about 25 miles from Fort Benning, Ga. on the top of a high hill. We sleep at night in our pup tents on the ground. We have to walk about a mile to take a shower or a swim. I take more swims than

*Sergeant Clifford Tompkins. Courtesy of Marie
B. Hardin.*

I do showers or else I take both. Last night I sat outside after dark playing poker + boy did the mosquitoes bite. I'll bet I killed a couple hundred. They can't get in our tents at night because we have a mosquito
net that fits just inside the tent.

The weather isn't nowheres near as hot here as it was in Fla. They say
we aren't going to stay here over a month. I don't know where we are
going from here. The rumor is that we are going to North Carolina +
from there up around N.Y., but that is only a rumor. I hope it is true.

We haven't done much of any work since we have been here + that
has been a week now Sunday.

We had a practice problem yesterday morning with tanks and planes.
You ought to see the new streamlined medium tanks + will they go.
Knock down trees a foot though we had 6 Aircobras + 4 light bombers

A20A's. Those Aircobras are fast. You hear + see them coming and just as quick they are gone. We had yesterday afternoon off. I took over a guy's K.P. for three bucks from 3 until 6 o-clock. I am taking one over today for $5.00 from 12:00 until 6:00 tonight.

Today is pay-day + everyone wants to leave or do something. I would go someplace myself but the nearest town is about 15 miles away + there will be so many soldiers in them that you can't turn around. I'll wait a couple of weeks + then go out. I draw about 80.00 today. Not bad for one month.

I expect to sell my car for $350 in a day or so. If the fellow that is going to buy it keeps his word. I think I told you that I had a car; well it is a 1938 Chev convertible, you know the same type as the Nash. It is way back down in Fla. now, 350 miles away. We aren't allowed to have one here so I think the best thing to do is sell.

I expected to have been home by this time but couldn't get a furlough. So it is hard to tell when I will be home now. I am all prepared to come home. Plenty of money + everything. This is just the time of year that I would like to be up there + get the feeling of old times again.

How is Clint? Do you see him much + is Bessie still at Harry's? In her last letter she said Harry + his wife quarrel more than ever. I guess it is in their blood. I guess that is all for now, so I will close hoping to hear from you soon + hope this finds you the same.

Clif

Fort Benning, Ga.
Sat. June 13, 42

Hello Reuben:

Received your nice long letter yesterday + was glad to hear that you are all well. Your letter as you ended it, did find me Coming Nearer

Home. We are leaving for Pennsylvania sometime next week. We were supposed to start Wednesday the 17th but something changed it. So maybe I will be able to get home before I expected.

I guess Bessie is going to stay at Harry's. She has been there for a couple of months, hasn't she?

Glad to hear that you have plenty of rain, but too much is about as bad as not enough. It poured rain here all afternoon yesterday. Came close to drowning us out of our tents. I hope it dries up a little so you can get to work again. I can see you are going to have a nice lot of spuds this year + a good hay crop.

Sunday

There was a thunderstorm last night. I never heard or saw such thunder + lightning in all my life. We haven't done any real drilling in so long. If they don't start pretty soon I will be so lazy that I can't do nothing.

We put on the big demonstration for the Generals. We practically had a real war. Four mortar shells fell right close to me + the rest of my Squad. One of them got a piece of steel from the first shell in his shoulder + and one finger half cut off + another got a hole through his canteen as big as a half dollar. That is all that happened to us but over all I think there was about 30 got hurt in the whole problem.

Clinton told me he was building a cow stable in the wagon house, but didn't give the details. It won't be long before you will be on your own when Russell takes his cows. Clinton told me in his last letter that he had 15 acres plowed I believe.

Those tanks weigh 28 tons. I don't know how many horsepower motors they have but the motor is just like an airplane motor. They will go about 60 miles an hour wide open but they only go about 30 through the woods + over rough ground. 28 tons going 25 or thirty miles an hour can knock down a lot.

Tuesday I saw a dive bomber crash + blow the three men in it into a million pieces. All there was is mince meat mixed up with pieces of the plane.

I sold my car Monday. Got a three day pass + went back to Stark where it was + sold it. Didn't get as much as it was worth but it was better than letting it sit down there. Maybe I will buy one when I come home + leave it with you to use when I come home. After the war it will be almost impossible to buy a car. Maybe I won't need one if I come as close to it as I did yesterday. There just didn't happen to be a piece of steel going my way but I got a face full of dirt.

Well I will have to bring this to a close hoping to be able to see you soon.

Clif

I'll let you know my new address as soon as I am sure.

So long.

• • •

Sgt. J. E. Williams was born on November 3, 1889, and became a supply sergeant serving in North Africa with the U.S. Army. When he enlisted, he had a wife and seven children, one of whom was also serving his country. Sergeant Williams wrote the following letter home to his son, Loren Williams of North Dakota, and it was contributed by Sergeant Williams's grandson, Bruce Williams of Washington. Sergeant Williams worked at many different jobs after the war, including supervisor of the disabled veterans irrigation project in the Burlington American Legion. In his later years, he worked for the Bank of North Dakota as a loan officer specializing in Veterans Administration loans. He spent most of his life trying to help veterans get the benefits they were due. After he retired, he was the county judge for Kidder County in North Dakota. He died of cancer in November 1975.

October 10, 1943

Hello little Major,

Cozy little wigwam, heated and lighted by the flame of a candle—raindrops playing tag on the roof and down the flaps. There are so many of them that they can't all crawl into the ground, so they pile up and dance around on the surface playing in the wind. They love to run, but only downhill, and the ground is level all around, so there's no place to go.

Sergeant J. E. Williams. Courtesy of Bruce Williams.

"Here comes a soldier," said one little raindrop, "let's hide in his shoe." "It's dark and he can't see us," said another, "see, he's slipping." "When he falls, we'll all jump into his pants pockets and stay there until the sun chases us out."

The soldier, being used to having little raindrops for company, didn't mind and goes on to his bunk, pulls his blanket tight around him, and

Sergeant J. E. Williams. Courtesy of Bruce Williams.

dreams of a little boy who used to hug him, and laugh, and say, "My Daddy,"—and of a white Christmas.

Then in the morning while it is still dark, he gets up and tramps through the mud some more. When daylight comes, the rain stops for awhile, and the soldier sees a beautiful rainbow. One end seemed to be just beyond the mountains, and the other end over there where you are. Mother Nature has built a beautiful bridge for him to go marching home on, and he starts out to look for its beginning beyond the mountain.

Good night and sweet dreams.

Love,

Daddy

• • •

Pfc. Andrew Martin Archer was born April 7, 1923, in Newark, New Jersey. He graduated from high school in 1941 then went to Cornell Univer-

sity in Ithaca, New York, for one year before enlisting in the U.S. Army on October 26, 1942. He served with the Ninety-second Quartermaster Company of the U.S. Army in Italy for twenty-seven months as a clerk doing morning reports, answering correspondence, completing forms, operating the switchboard, and taking and sending calls for the company as assistant vehicle dispatcher. He received the American Theater Ribbon, the European–African–Middle Eastern Ribbon, the Good Conduct Medal, and the Victory Medal. As an African-American, Private First Class Archer wrote home to New York of prejudices he faced in the military. His daughter, Betty Hopkins of California, who contributed her father's letter, says that "OM" refers to Private First Class Archer's father's nickname, Old Master; his son was called Young Master. After his discharge on January 4, 1946, Private First Class Archer went to school at the Manhattan Technical Institute, the City College of New York, and Columbia University. He became an engineer and an inventor, doing research with laser beams and developing ways to record breaks in the beams. He died on May 2, 1967, in an automobile accident.

June 13, 1944

Dear Dad,

Is that your natural odor or have you been pulling your suspenders out of the toilet some more? How's OM today? I'm okay, though raising no hell. Was just looking sadly out of the window at the big fire in the mountains that we're going to have to work on tonight, on our own time of course. The CO wouldn't think of letting us go up now, not on GI time, and the damn thing is spreading.

Work is pretty slow around the office right now. It's given me lots of time to dig into that calculus some more. By the way, when are you sending that book? It was really on the ball. What I regret is not having a chance to use it as much as I wanted to during the A.S.T.P. training.

Private First Class Andrew Martin Archer.
Courtesy of Betty Hopkins.

Speaking of the A.S.T.P., I was over to the classification office to try to get the forms I told you about and was told that the reactivated A.S.T.P. was closed to the 92nd Division. Some shit! Now I know why they put all the colored in this outfit. Don't worry, the ol boy hasn't quit yet. I'm putting in my application regardless. The O.C.S. board should be convening soon also. I understand it has been selected already.

Did you send in the request for your credits, and if so, what was the outcome? I'm jumping right back in the school for a year or so at gov't. expense as soon as this war is over. It can't last but so long in the European theatre. Of course we may wind up in Burma, China, and possibly Tokyo, but it can't last much longer even with the Asiatic war going on.

Private First Class Andrew Martin Archer (top left with arms resting on knee) with troop. Courtesy of Betty Hopkins.

After all the times I've worked in the Chemical Warfare Section and put companies after companies through chlorine, tear gas, chloropic-trin, mustard, and practically every other gas, and rode around hours trying to get the stuff out of clothes, they tell me I'm not P.O.M. qualified, and [I] had to go through the gas chamber yesterday. One cat in our group started popping like one of those T model Fords, and every time we holler "Gas" around him now he takes off like a jackrabbit. He had to be taken to the dispensary for treatment. You see the dope (a master sgt.) couldn't understand how the lecturing officer in the gas chamber could hold his breath and talk to us at the same time without feeling the effects of the gas, so he thought he'd try it. He soon found out that the trick was to take a deep breath before attempting to talk.

How's the job and all the cats on it? Give everyone my regards.

Love,
YM

. . .

First Lt. Thomas Haynes Marnette served with the U.S. Army, 168th Infantry Regiment, Thirty-fourth Infantry Division, Company I, in North Africa and was killed in Fondouk Pass in Tunisia on April 7, 1943. His daughter, Diane Marnette Sagen of California, who shared her father's letter, says it was written after his landing at Fedhala near Casablanca.

Sunday, Nov. 15, 1942

My darling:

Happy anniversary! See. I didn't forget—even with all the running around I've been doing. And before I go any further—I love you—and love you—and miss you terribly. Don't know quite where to begin to tell you about this—I've got censorship regulations down pretty well, but there's so much I'd like to say that I can't.

Anyway, we're in Casablanca—after a hellish week. Somebody was evidently pretty peeved at us for landing—and threw a lot of stuff at us—but I ducked so they missed me. I got cut up a little while swimming, but I'm perfectly ok. This past week has no coherence—no pattern, in my recollections, but is just a series of impressions. And I'll try to give you those I can remember—and those I am permitted.

First—I know how a fly feels caught in a spider web. Very much the same as I felt when their searchlights on shore came on and caught our boat. Dodge as you will, you can't escape it—and then the little red dots start coming toward you, and over you, and you find that it is, after all, possible to be down in the bottom of the boat, even if you were crowded standing. And then you hit shore—(we hit on a coral reef—needle sharp and fantastically carved by surf) and get out and start ashore, wondering what's coming. Then—wham! it comes. And you hug the rocks or sand and try to get under it.

Fortunately, the native garrison and many of the French surrendered at Fedhala soon after we landed. (Fedhala is 17 miles N of Casablanca.) But we were sniped, and relentlessly shelled by batteries on the Cape, and had all in all quite a time of it.

But even during a time like that there are impressions—a French battery, with shells pounding in on it, bravely returning the fire until a direct hit smashes it—natives frantically herding families, goats, camels and donkeys out to the country—red-fezzed Moroccan troops, coming up to surrender, smiling at us—the group of sullen German officers we caught at Hotel Miramar, and the coffee and native bread offered me—and accepted with great thanks—by a black-skinned Moroc in uniform.

There is a conglomeration of everything in Morocco. Smells, especially. The towns are pungent with garlic, camels and people. You must see a native quarter to believe it. Joseph's coat of many colors has nothing on the average Arab, who merely sews another patch to the place where the old one was. Their rags literally hang on them, how, I don't know. They swarm all over you, begging "cigarres, choon-gum, shoc-lut."

After the beautiful gardens of Fedhala—the country to Casablanca was pretty rough. Dry and bare—and open—except when you came to occasional farms. These farms are marvels. They are villas—most beautiful homes and richly decorated, and each with its own squalid native section walled in. In the U.S. these homes would represent an expenditure of $85–90,000—and what they grow here to justify the outlay I don't know. The hills are not fertile or cultivated, except rarely—there are, however, extensive orange and lemon groves. Item: While we were digging in to protect ourselves—I looked away about 200 yards and saw a native, plowing unconcernedly with a camel—paying no attention whatever to the shells coming down 100 yards away.

Casablanca was tough. But they were glad to see us when it was all over. They're game fighters—and grand people, les Francais. I went in to the city rather early on a mission—and the troops were being mobbed by the most joyous crowd I have ever seen. That is not propaganda. These people felt freed of a definite oppression. But I never felt less like a conquering hero. There was, of course, a considerable amount of damage on both sides. Anyway—here is an unusual town. A mixture of races, customs and architecture. A Moslem burial ground, with walls ancient before America became the U.S., right next to a modern brewery. Street vendors in rags, selling nuts and tomatoes by the Shell building—an edifice that makes Frank Lloyd Wright seem conservative. Carriages of all kinds, drawn by beautiful horses, and always the jangle of bicycle bells. A lot of restaurants—but very little food. Cigarettes, sugar are rationed. Meat? What is it? Two years ago they had chocolate. The shops are nearly cleaned out—looted by the departing Germans. But I met a refugee Pole who spoke English, and he took some of us to a small place where we had dinner prepared by—"Andre," formerly of the Roosevelt Hotel in New York!

I am living—as liaison officer to the next higher unit—in what was probably the chapel of a private house. Before my bedroll got here I folded up a rug which is probably worth $600—and slept on it. This room is small—about 20 × 30. Inlaid marble floor, tile walls to shoulder height, and then alabaster lace fresco to the ceiling. The ceiling is a riot of oriental splendor. These huge alabaster chandeliers hang from deep wells in the ceiling, and are equipped with two sets of lights—one shining through soft blue glass, and another set lighting up red and yellow.

Another set of lights illumines the windows, also of alabaster lacework and colored glass. The doors are heavy hand-carved and painted wood. The house has its own swimming pool—dry—and tennis courts.

In the main house all the doors are heavy plate glass. The stairs—inside and out—are pinkish marble—and the bathrooms ultra modern white tile—but no hot water. The gardens are exquisite. Guess all in all the best description would be a cross between Grauman's Orient theatre and the Hearst Home at Santa Monica. Except that here it is all in excellent taste. But we eat our canned rations here just the same—and I took probably the coldest bath in history here—and loved it. And if this is paradise—the flies are terrific. And the lights go out at the damnedest times.

Everybody wants a. to be friendly, b. cigarettes, c. chewing gum, d. chocolate. In about that order. My supply of gum and chocolate was ruined when I swam ashore, so even I miss that. Wine is 7 francs a bottle, but still not a steak in town. A franc is worth 1¼ cents at present.

Lest it appear that I'm having a whee of a time, let me say that I'm not. I'm working, and it is not pleasant wondering when some malcontent is going to whang a rifle bullet at you at nite. There has been some sniping, and one nite several of us spent an interesting hour out hunting and being hunted. But they are becoming much less active. The gendarmes are doing splendid work. And frankly, I'm a bit tired of C Ration, which has been my only food for 8 days—except for the one exception I noted. Meat and beans—vegetable hash—and meat and beans. Served by myself in opulent splendor—but still—meat and beans.

And my darling, how are you? I wonder so much about you. The pictures of you are almost literally worn out—the case got pretty wet and came apart, but your pictures are unharmed. And during a lull I got them out to look at them—and discovered your verse on the back— "How do I love thee? Let me count the ways."

It's by Elizabeth Barrett Browning, n'est-ce pas? And very lovely.

Anyway, afterwards I could have taken Casablanca by myself.

And little Tommy? Or little Kathryn? Or whoever?

How are you two getting along? Darling—I miss you so darn much.

Please take good care of both of you—and let me know. And you must not worry at all—but remain sure that God will help both of us to be together again.

Have you got an apartment? Where are you? And how are you? And, O my beloved, I love you so much.

How are all the folks? I can't write to them just yet—so you'll have to act as relay messenger. But give them all my love—and ask them to help us along over here. We need all your help—and we'll fix up this job.

There's no news too trivial to be interesting from home! Here small things assume great proportions. We'd do anything for a bath—or clean clothes. Toilet paper is hoarded and the fortunate individual who has any is a lucky soldier. Ink? I'm writing with ersatz hurriedly left behind by the German staff.

Now darling, will you do something for your far-away husband? Please send me clippings on what the papers said about us, and if you can promote some Hershey bars and chewing gum—I'd love it. 5 lbs is the limit you can send, but it'd make a swell gift from you. And pictures too—I want to know all about you—and the family. Even if I can't write to them—I think about them and miss them.

Now I'll quit—and write another letter which I shall enclose for you to forward—because you'll have the right address. I have never hated to write a letter more in my life—and you'll understand why. But we have already become reconciled to such things—and we take it—and fight harder because of it. I would have done anything in the world to have prevented it, but that's the hellish part of this business.

Anyway—help Carolyn along, will you honey? And keep always within you that faith that you have, and the rest of us will know it—and come back to all of you at home.

Goodnite, darling—and I love you—more than ever.

Your husband,
Tom

I don't know my address—but I think it's on my safe arrival card which you should have rec'd. Darling: If you don't think this letter should go just yet, hold it until you want to send it. Thanks.

• • •

David James Weepers was a navigator with the Royal Canadian Air Force, 625th Squadron, Royal Air Force located at Kelstern, England. He wrote the following letter to his wife a few days before he was shot down in northern Belgium. Officer Weepers's daughter, Donna Niewinski of Ontario, Canada, who shared this letter, says that her father's Lancaster was shot down May 22, 1944, near Meer, Belgium, and that the pilot and copilot died in the crash. He was able to parachute out safely and traveled through the Belgian resistance line (Kadar line) until July 22, 1944, when he was captured by the Germans in Antwerp. He remained in Luft 1 in Barth until May 13, 1945, and he returned home safely after the war.

May 16, 1944

Dear Doreen:

Hello darling, here's another one for you and I think I'm right on time with this one for a change. I think I wrote my last one about five days ago, but seeing as I received no less than three from you yesterday I thought I'd better not lose any time in getting one off to you.

So you got a laugh out of me travelling 9 miles to spend 75 minutes with my blonde, eh! Well, I had a bit of a laugh over it myself. Don't know what's so funny about my explanation of T.T.F.N. but I guess maybe I should read my letters more closely after I write them. Please tell me what was so funny about it all.

Sorry about the pictures honey, but Jack Duncan, the guy that took them, hasn't sent me any prints yet so therefore you haven't received some. As soon as I get them, they'll be on the way to you.

David James Weepers.
Courtesy of Donna Niewinski.

Please forgive my last couple of letters, blaming you about not receiving any mail from you honey. As I said before, I got three yesterday, dated April 22, 26 and 29, so I realize you are really looking after me. On Monday, I also received your swell parcel and believe me dear I was the happiest guy on the station. You talk about me not telling you what I need, but I ask you how could anyone improve on such a selection of stuff as you sent in that box. I also received a "mickey" of stuff the same day (from my other girlfriend), so I'm all set for a party now, or on second thought, maybe I should save it for a couple weeks when I go on leave again and share it with my blonde 9 miles from London HA! HA! Honestly dear that parcel of yours was the best I ever received; you're a darling.

So you are going back to work for the old firm, eh? Well, that is really something. If I remember correctly, my friend Mr. Sims is Transport Controller and a pretty good egg I think. Don't forget to give my best to all the old gang that are still around the place and lots of luck to you.

Well honey, maybe you have noticed that this letter is a bit depressing, but it can't be helped, it's just the way I feel. I worked last night, and my best friend in the mess, outside of Max, was among those who didn't come back. I don't know what could have happened to him and his crew—they were one of the best crews on the station—but as I have often said before it's about 90% luck in this business anyway. Last night made it 19 for me and it was a tough one. I don't think I ever felt so scared in all my life as I did last night and I've really been scared a few times before. Last night was my first trip in about 6 days and do you know it is harder to get down to business after a long layoff like that than it is when you go every night. Right now honey I feel like starting in and going every night until I get the next dozen or so in and finishing this tour. I think eleven more will do it, and I hope it won't take much more than another month.

Jeez, I'm almost frozen writing this to you. Last week we had beautiful weather—a couple of days like summer—but yesterday it turned cold and started to rain and it has been that way ever since. With no fires allowed (to conserve coal) it is impossible to get warm except in the air and that's the truth. Last night it was a treat to go on "ops" just to feel the heat in the aircraft.

Well I see it is 7:30 and time for dinner so I guess the rest of this will have to wait until I eat.

Sorry dear, here it is 11 p.m. and I'm just finishing up this letter. I got so damned cold in the mess that I got hold of Max and the two of us came down to the hut, stole some coke and we have a lovely fire going now. We have just finished a snack from your swell parcel and Max has rolled into bed thoroughly content with himself and I don't expect to hear anything from him until sometime tomorrow morning. I'm just sitting here looking at your pictures dear, two of them, in your fur coat. I've got them pinned up on the dresser, and yes I wish you wuz here honey. Here's two of the crew just arrived so I guess I won't get to sleep for another couple of hours, and its a hell of a good job I'm almost through with this letter because I'll never be able to write with this riot going on here. So honey, I guess I'll close off for another time hoping you are getting these letters of mine and keep up the good work from your end.

Lots of love,
Dave

. . .

The following letter was written by Maj. Howard ("Hitch") Brigham, who was operations officer for the 345th Bombardment Group (Medium), the "Air Apaches." For additional biographical information about Major Brigham, please see Part I: The Battles—By Air.

Somewhere in New Guinea
(Dammit)
39 Missions
154 Combat Hours
May 9, 1944

Dear Dad,

I haven't heard much from home lately. What is the matter? Was the wedding too much for everyone? I did get one from Bob and Fran on their honeymoon. From what Bob says you were having such a good time at the reception that you thought they ought to stay instead of going on their honeymoon. Is that true or just an ugly rumor?

A week ago I took a fat cat down to Cairns to pick up some supplies. It was a nice break in the routine. We took off early in the morning and got

Major Howard Brigham. Courtesy of Robert C. Flint.

there in time to make the noon opening of the pubs. That cold beer sure tasted good. It made me hungry as well as a little buzzy and I ate two huge steaks that noon along with several glasses of milk and polished the meal off with a piece of chocolate pie and two scoops of ice cream. Had only one steak for supper though. I dug up three cases of beer, a case of sherry, a case of gin and whiskey including one bottle of Scotch and some other things I needed and so you can see it was an all-around successful trip for me. Needless to say I have lots of friends these days.

When we first got here the food was pretty bad but now it is better than average. Instead of losing the weight I put on in Sydney I am afraid I am keeping it. We gave a ride up here to a couple of Navy Lts. and in the process of getting acquainted I found out that one had been a very good friend of Pete Warren at Harvard. His name was Bob White and he also knew Dwight Ellis, the Burbanks and some others. They stayed with us for a few days before going on and we showed them a pretty good time. Our club for once had some liquor and so we put on a party. For some reason all the pilots around here take a great delight in buzzing our area and they got a big bang out of that. I told them I would take them up and show them a real buzz job so the next day we got a new ship, one equipped like the ones in the article you once sent me, and set out for some fun. We went out and fired the cannon and they were really amazed at such a huge piece of armament in an airplane. We got right on the deck on the way back and when we went over a point of land we had to pull up to go over the trees. Next we went up to 5,000 feet and played around in the clouds. I would dive the ship to about 300 mph and then pull up into a steep climb and stand it on a wing on top of the climb and then let the nose drop into another dive. It was great sport and I was tempted to roll it over on its back and do a Split S but a B-25 isn't made for that. I got as much kick out of it as they did and they decided a B-25 was a pretty good ship. They didn't realize that a bomber could be kicked around like that. My engineer said I must have thought it was a P-25. Gotta go to chow now. Write soon.

Love.

. . .

Pvt. Arthur E. Stark was nineteen-years-old and a senior in high school when he enlisted in the Army. He entered the service in April 1943 and sailed for overseas duty in October. He was stationed in North Africa and later in Italy with the 143rd Infantry. On January 21, 1944, he was instructed to carry the battalion switchboard across the Rapido River in conjunction with an attack against the enemy. Enemy artillery, mortar, and machine gun fire fell around him, but he remained at his post for three days, even after the battalion was forced to withdraw. He received shrapnel wounds and died five days later. Private Stark was posthumously awarded the Purple Heart and Silver Star. The following letter was written by him and sent to his then-eleven-year-old sister, Carole Joyce Stark Blocker of Tennessee, who contributed it to this collection.

Private Arthur E. Stark. Courtesy of Carole Joyce Stark Blocker.

To: Miss Carole Joyce Stark
Hendersonville, Tennessee

From: Pvt Arthur E. Stark
H.Q. Co., 2nd Bat. 143 I.
A.P.O. 36th P=_NY NY

Jan 2, 1944

Dear Doll Doll,

I just wrote to Mamma, Margaret, and Lucille so I thought you would get mad if I didn't write you so I'll try to think of something to say. I used to think a v-mail was the thing to write on but they are the biggest things to fill up you ever saw. Did you have a big Christmas? You should have seen mine. I guess I'm lucky that the little boys and girls over here didn't have much Christmas. They had their buckets out in our chow line begging for something to eat. It's really pitiful the way they were treated before we got over here. Almost all of them wore G.I. clothing that was given them or they stole someplace. I sure wouldn't want this to happen to anybody back home. Well if you can understand this it's OK but I guess you can—after all, you're my <u>sister</u>. Ha Ha. Well, write when you can.

Love,
Sticks

. . .

Cpl. Franklin M. Elliott served in Company A of the 741st Tank Battalion, which landed at 6:30 A.M. on D day on Omaha Beach. The men in his battalion were fated to be part of the initial assault wave. Corporal Elliott landed on the "Easy Red" sector of Omaha Beach, and he died later in the day near the bluff, according to his daughter, DeRonda Elliott of North Carolina, who shared her father's letters. Ms. Elliott is a member of AWON, the American War Orphans Network.

March 4, 1944

Dearest Polly,

It amazes even your husband that in all my writing to you I have never mentioned the one thing that affects my life most deeply; ie. the Army chow line. This phenomenon quite resembles a snake. A long, coiling, many-vertebraed snake. To the distant observer the rattler is brought to mind due to the continual rattle and hiss coming therefrom. There are in this coiling line every manner of dogface goldbrick (up front) chowhound, and boot polisher in the Army. I know one fellow who has a photo of a chow line with an officer (a 2nd Looey) standing about mid-way through with mess gear in hand. This is such a rarity that he has been offered thousands by the Smithsonian and the London Museum for the negative thereof. Me? I'm just another one of the vertebra previously mentioned. It causes me to say that I'd wait a century just for your burnt biscuits.

Frank

[Excerpt]

April 4, 1944

Hi Polly,

Sometimes the water is hot but most of the time it is cold as it is at the present moment, so I'll try again tomorrow and maybe get a shower. England turned the clock ahead again so we are saving daylight savings—two hours ahead of the sun. They can stop that clock as far as I am concerned until the war is over. Everything is at a standstill in my life as long as this abominable Army stands between the two of us. Everybody in the Army gripes about doing more work than the other guy. That makes for a very humorous dialogue because there isn't a guy in the Army who does enough work to make what he earns. If the expression that a good army is one that gripes is true then Hitler better give up right away because this is the world's best army along these lines. . . .

Frank

• • •

Pfc. C. Robert Milgate wrote the following letters to Pauline Milgate, his wife, and his two children, Sharon and Gary, who were both under two years old while he was stationed in Europe. Private First Class Milgate served in the U.S. Army from July 24, 1944, to February 26, 1946, and was a member of the 289th Infantry of the Seventy-fifth Division, Company C. He fought in the Battle of the Bulge in the European theater of war with the Ninth Army. His military occupations were basic infantry, rifleman, light mortar crewman, and heavy truck driver. He earned the European–African–Middle Eastern Service Medal, the Good Conduct Medal, and the World War II Victory Medal. He was awarded the Combat Infantryman's Badge while in Europe. His battalion was also awarded the Bronze Star for fighting under fire in the Battle of the Bulge. After V-E Day, May 9, 1945, he returned to Camp Oklahoma City in Reims France, where he worked in the motor pool, driving heavy equipment. He returned to the United States on the George Washington *and entered port on February 22, 1946, George Washington's birthday. He was discharged from Fort Dix, New Jersey, on February 26, 1946. The following letter was submitted by his daughter, Cindy Knoblauch of Florida, on behalf of Private First Class C. Robert Milgate's wife.*

Somewhere in Germany
19–April–45
75th Div. 9th Army

Dearest Wife and Babies:

Another day is gone by and one day closer to the end. Received the papers and a couple of v-mails from the folks. Did you happen to see a photograph in any of the newspapers of a sign painted on a wall which reads as follows: "Roses are red, violets are blue, the 289th took Ickeren too." If you did get a copy or can get a copy with it in, hang on to it.

We got our PX rations today. The most we have received at one time since I've been over here. We got 9 Clark bars, 5 Necco wafers, 3 cigars, 6 packs of gum, a can of orange juice, 2 big cans of peanuts and a face towel. Every man got this much. Everyone is pretty well satisfied this

Private First Class C. Robert Milgate with his wife, Pauline, and his two oldest children, Sharon and Gary, which was taken when he was on furlough after his son was born. Courtesy of Cynthia Knoblauch.

evening. This is a pretty nice place here where we are. We have electricity and have liberated a radio so it's quite a change from what we've been having. We get quite a number of good programs thru the AEF, American Expeditionary Forces. We heard the Hit Parade, Bob Hope and tonite Frank Morgan's program. So we keep pretty well up on our music. We get the news every hour from the front lines but even that is 24 hours old. We know we're still advancing toward Berlin. Went to the show tonite. The title was "A Song to Remember." It was in technicolor and was pretty good. It was the first we have seen since we left the Rhine.

See by the *Spectator* that brother Willy was AWOL when he got back to San Francisco. He'll be shipped out on the next boat though. You can

Private First Class C. Robert Milgate (first row, second from left) with weapons platoon, 75th Division, 289th Infantry, Company C. Courtesy of Cynthia Knoblauch.

bet on that. Hate to see him go over into the South Pacific though. That's a hell of a lot worse than it is over here from all reports. Let me know how he makes out.

How's everything at home, honey? Mother said that they would be putting in their garden soon so must be you have been having some good weather. I hope you have anyway. I know I sure dreaded winter. It always seemed to hang on so long in the spring.

Never have wrote to Thelma's folks yet but am going to keep trying. I'll make it one [of] these days in the near future.

Guess I'd better close and catch some shut-eye. Write me some news of my babes, bum. Until then—so long.

As Ever Your Loving Husband and Daddy,

Bob

. . .

Capt. Lillard E. Pratt served with the 343rd Field Artillery, Ninetieth Division, U.S. Army. He was killed by an eighty-eight-millimeter shell on February 22, 1945, while serving as volunteer liaison officer for Col. William Dupuy, Third Army, under General George S. Patton, at the battle for Lictenberg, Germany. His wife, Pauline E. Spence of Nebraska, shared his letter.

December 13, 1944

My Lovers Pauline, Dave and John:

Your old fat Daddy sends his love again. Not again, but forever.

We are having a plenty tough time just now. The battle for Germany is much more savage than Normandy ever thought of being. Here we have a more dangerous enemy in the weather than actual bullets. Some soldiers have trench foot so bad they can barely get their bare feet into overshoes. These men will all lose their feet. War is terrible at its best, but at its worst it is a living and dying hell. Someday, however, the guns will stop booming and we can clear the battlefield and go home.

Don't think my spirits are low because I know such a condition is like death itself, so I force myself to keep my chin up. And it is possible to search hard enough to find a bright ray of hope. I know we are going to win, and that itself must keep us going.

Lover, it is time for chow so I will close with love for all.

All my love,
Daddy

P.S. Did you ever get my surprise? It was a picture of myself. Will enclose another just in case the first got lost.

PART V

Away from Home—

Impressions of New Lands

Lt. Stanley Joshua Jacobs was born in September 1916, in New York City, grew up in Jacksonville, Florida, and was working a sales job in Chicago to escape the tropical climate that caused his chronic asthma when he received his draft notice at the end of 1942. After completing the U.S. Army's "ninety day wonder" officer candidate course at Fort Benning, Georgia, in 1942, he was assigned to the 305th Regimental Combat Team of the Seventy-seventh Infantry Division as a rifle platoon leader. He met and married his wife, Alice, in 1943 while the Seventy-seventh was training in Arizona but soon had to leave when the division was ordered into combat in the Pacific. The Seventy-seventh Division participated in combat operations on Guam, Leyte, Kerama Retto, and Okinawa. Lieutenant Jacobs was severely wounded during the fighting on Ie Shima, a small island off the coast of Okinawa. The day after Lieutenant Jacobs's injury, war correspondent Ernie Pyle, who was visiting the Seventy-seventh Division, was killed there. Lieutenant Jacobs wrote the first of the two following letters home to his mother during the Battle of Guam, which began on July 21, 1944. Japan had invaded and occupied the lightly defended island of Guam concurrently with the attack on Pearl Harbor. American Marines and the Seventy-seventh Infantry Division liberated Guam in the summer of 1944, and the island was declared secure on August 10, 1944. The

Seventy-seventh departed Guam for Leyte, in the Philippine Islands, on November 3, 1944. Lieutenant Jacobs wrote the second letter during the Battle of Leyte. The Seventy-seventh Division landed at Leyte in November 1944, and participated in combat operations on the island until February 1945. After spending a year in the hospital recovering from his combat injuries, Jacobs attended the University of California, Berkeley, on the G.I. Bill and earned undergraduate and graduate degrees. He became a college teacher in the San Francisco Bay area. He died in 1987 as the result of complications from his war injury. Both letters were contributed by Lieutenant Jacobs's son, Mike Jacobs of California, from the estate of Stanley Joshua Jacobs.

Lieutenant Stanley Jacobs. Courtesy of Michael D. Jacobs.

Somewhere in the Pacific
October 8, 1944

Dear Mom,

The enclosed article appeared in "Yank" magazine. As the article states, we were the first to contact the natives and I was right there when they came toward our lines. It is hard to describe how we felt when that happened. We had been fighting several days by then and we had not seen anyone except the Japs we had killed. The author puts it very well when he tells the comment of one soldier. It was a lot more than that also. To me it seemed that at last there was some tangible evidence that the war was worth fighting.

We first saw them late one afternoon—a long thin line of them. One of our patrols headed the column and was leading them into our area. The column of people just seemed endless. As they came closer we saw them, the old, the sick, children, men, women, everybody. Those who could not walk were being carried. All were in tattered clothing; some carried a few cherished possessions. The only possession of many was a crucifix. Many had small American flags which they waved. They must have kept them hidden all the time the Japs were here. Then as they got to us they laughed and shook hands with everyone and we had a hard time keeping them from stopping and not moving back to a place that was safe.

Suddenly we all seemed to have a lump in our throat as we watched and talked to that seemingly endless line of people. They seemed to have just one thought, to get to where the Americans were and then all their troubles would be over.

When they got close to us their faces would just light up and they just didn't know what to do to show us how they felt. Many of the men wanted guns and wanted to go with us and we did use many as guides who went with us through the rest of the fight. Those who were with my Battalion proved invaluable. They were willing to do anything for us. One of the native boys was with my platoon. He got coconuts for us, showed us how to use bamboo, coconut leaves and lots of stuff while we had to live in the field.

There are many new experiences in combat but that is one of the pleasantest ones I shall never forget.

As you see, the foregoing was my reason for this letter. You owe me one letter as I write this; maybe it's on the way. Hope you are well and everything is going good at school. I'm fine and hear from Alice regularly. She is okay too. Write me soon as I sure look forward to mail call around here.

Your loving son,
Stan

Somewhere in the Philippines
February 22, 1945

Darling Alice,

I don't feel like writing much today. However, I think about you and know you want to hear from me. Yesterday I wrote to the mother of one of my men who was killed on Leyte. I took almost all day to write that letter. I thought very hard about what to say that would help her bear the loss of her beloved son. This morning we had a memorial service for the men of our regiment who fell on Leyte. Colonel Tanzola said that if the dead had one wish they could convey to us, it would be for us to carry on and see that they did not die in vain. He is right.

I saw a funny sight today. You girls at home, we hear, can't get enough silk hose but I saw a native girl who had found one of our parachutes somewhere and had made a very nice looking silk dress out of it. Across the back of it in big stamped letters it said "Inspected and passed by U.S. Army quartermaster inspector."

Honey, I close now with all my love to you.

Your boy,
Stan

• • •

Mary Edith Engle was one of the select few women to become a WASP, a member of the Women Airforce Service Pilots. According to her daughter, Nancy Engle of Ohio, who contributed her mother's letter, nearly 25,000 women applied for service in the WASPs, but only 1,830 were accepted for training, and only 1,074 earned their wings. Mary Edith Engle was one of those few. She signed up in 1942 and was in the fourth class to graduate, Class 43-W-4, on August 7, 1943, at Avenger Field in Sweetwater, Texas. Ms. Engle was stationed in Dallas, Texas, after she earned her wings, and she ferried planes all over the country—mostly untested aircraft sent directly from the factories to military airfields—until the WASPs were disbanded on December 20, 1944.

The WASPs were not considered official military at that time, so they were not given a rank, but they were the first women in the history of America authorized to fly military aircraft. They had to pay for their own funerals if they were killed in the line of duty. Ms. Engle had to pay her own way to get back home. For more than thirty years the records from the bases where the WASPs were stationed were locked in U.S. archives and marked "Top Secret." It wasn't until 1979, thirty-five years after they were demobilized, that Congress declared them to be official veterans of World War II. Ms. Engle was inducted into the Kentucky Aviation Hall of Fame in 1996.

[Undated]
Sunday

Dear Mother,

I'm still on my way to Canada. I'm as far as Medford, Oregon now. We sat in Sacramento from last Saturday night till Friday. We finally got out, went 125 miles to Red Bluff & had to land. Yesterday we started to Seattle, ran into weather & landed at Medford. Little by little we're getting there. I found a little vase last night I thought would make a nice valentine for you. I hope it isn't smashed by the time you get it.

Mary Edith Engle showing new wings. Courtesy of Nancy Engle Gordon.

Yesterday I really saw a beautiful sight. We left Red Bluff & climbed up to 10,000 ft. to clear the mountains. The clouds under us kept getting thicker until they were just a solid white mass under me & the sky so blue above & Mt. Shasta was peeping out but it was covered with snow so it was just a blue & white world. I was flying along for about an hour & it was beginning to look as if I'd have to let down through the clouds & that's no fun. I was beginning to get a little worried when I saw a hole in the clouds. I scooted through & found the only field for two hundred miles & it was the only break in the clouds. I got through, said, "Thanks, God, I'll take it now" & landed. Isabel found the same spot & came in too. Five minutes later the hole closed in. See why there are no atheists in the skies?

We've been sitting all day waiting for it to clear here but no luck. We hope to get out tomorrow. It's been so long since I've had any mail I'm wondering if Lexington is still there. We are in the officers club now & there's an awful lot of flying going on. You really hear some wild tales. I can hardly wait to see Canada. It's surprising how warm it is here. I guess it's 'cause we are so close to the Pacific. We've got to be out by sunrise tomorrow so I guess we'd better get to bed.

Love,
Mary Edith

• • •

Dr. Robert Andrew Douglas served in the Australian Army Medical Corps from December 1940 until October 1946. For additional biographical information, please refer to Part I: The Battles.

27 January '42

Dear Mother and Father,

Many thanks for your last letters, they have been arriving quite regularly. As you may have gathered from my last letter I am in Syria now and like the place very well—much better than Palestine. The Arabs here are mostly Christian in this part of the country and most of them are not really Arabs at all. There is not so much dirt and none of the eternal wailing for backsheesh. They are very poor but have a tremendous pride in themselves, they like the Australians very much and will give you anything. The villages are built of stone and the houses are well furnished. I was out billeted in a house for a fortnight and we all formed quite a friendship with the proprietor and his family. At the present time I am assisting in running a military hospital in one of the large towns. It is a beautiful hospital built by the Italians as a sort of propaganda measure I think, though the place was staffed by the Carmelite sisters—so there are holy pictures all over the place. It was taken over by the French first and then by ourselves. Our quarters are very comfortable and hot and cold laid-on from chip heaters. Part of the horizon is taken up by towering snow covered mountains—they are only about ten miles away but fortunately it is not very cold here.

Jim spent one night here so I got the word and came in from the country where I was then stationed and tried to find him. Eventually I located him bedded down in a stable; it was like trying to find a needle in a haystack. He looks very well and is back to almost his old girth. He told me of some hair-raising experiences he had in Tobruk. He was occupying an old Italian post on the Tobruk perimeter and the Huns bombarded and then attacked. He managed to beat them off but our side thought the post captured so our artillery shelled it, then the Germans shelled it again knowing it wasn't captured and then one of our tanks kept running round shelling it with a small cannon. He should have got a decoration as there were 20 dead Germans outside the place. The chap who got the MC had only one outside his post but he had a slight wound and told a better story.

Bob

26 September '43

Dear Mother and Father,

Many thanks for your letters which are arriving quite regularly. The lighter flints have proved an absolute godsend.

We are now allowed to tell officially that we are in New Guinea and that we have been in action. The veil of censorship has been somewhat lifted. I am now sitting in the middle of a jungle on my rustic bed penning this letter to the accompaniment of a bombardment, ours thank goodness. This used to be Japanese territory but they did not put up much of a fight for it. In fact I may consider myself now to be an experienced jungle soldier. I will not tell you how we got here but you can figure it out for yourselves but it was certainly a most hair-raising experience.

So far as my limited experience goes I am of the opinion that I would much rather be in a war here than in Egypt. It is not very hot, milder than the NQ [i.e., North Queensland] summer by far. It rains fairly frequently but one soon gets to know how to keep moderately dry. There is always plenty of running water and a lot of shade. In fact but for the war it is quite a pleasant place. Other campaigns may have been different but I think the horrible stories about NG [i.e., New Guinea] have been grossly exaggerated.

As for the Japs, all the troops have the opinion that he is a lousy soldier which is indeed true. He seems to lack all tactical sense and has been driven out of positions that our troops could have held against vastly superior numbers. I don't know whether their troops are second class or not but they certainly seem like it, they have run like hell every time and as for this infiltration business, well, he doesn't leave any troops behind let alone try to attack us. The jungle gives him every opportunity to ambush us etc. but he very seldom tries it on. His artillery is very poor and ours makes life a perfect hell for him as he does not like HE [i.e., High Explosive]. He inflicts very few casualties on us even when cornered and then he goes into a panic and commits hari-kari by holding a grenade to his head and pulling the pin which procedure is convenient to all concerned. However his Air Force seems pretty good and when his bombers get through they bomb very accurately from a height of about 15,000 to 20,000 feet so that you cannot tell when or where the bombs are going to land. Any AA fire at all always makes him stick for high altitudes.

Hugh was quite well last time I saw him about a week ago. His company had a sticky job a while back but Hugh managed to come through without danger.

Your loving son,
Bob

• • •

Sgt. Gilbert ("Buster") Machette enlisted in the New Jersey National Guard, "Essex Troop," which was known as the 102nd Reconnaisance Cavalry

Squadron (Mechanized). In January 1941, Buster went to England, where he spent the next nineteen months. The 102nd Cavalry Reconnaisance Squadron landed on Omaha Beach two days after D day, on June 8, 1944. There they joined with the First Infantry Division to advance on the beach and to protect the flank of the V Corps. The 102nd then led the Fourth Infantry Division into Paris. Six days after his last letter to his sister, dated August 18, 1944, Buster was killed when his platoon encountered an enemy ambush. Buster's nephew, Edward Morrows of New Jersey, who contributed his letter, tells the following story: "War not only took Buster from his loved ones but it stole the solace of closure to his death. His family was told that he had been killed in St. Lô, France, and his parents gave instructions to the Army to bury their son in France: 'Let him lie where he fell.' The Army confirmed the request, and their wishes were carried out—Buster was buried in St. Lô. After that, life went on, but it was a life where no one smiled or laughed. Florence's husband, Walter [Buster's brother-in-law], was in the infantry, and in 1944 he was going through France. He knew his wife's brother was buried in the St. Lô Cemetery. When he had the opportunity to go there, he did; he wanted to see Buster's grave. Walt searched and couldn't find it. He went to the groundskeepers, and after checking the records, he found that there was no one there by the name of Gilbert Machette. Neither Florence nor Walter understood this, but Florence said nothing to her parents. She didn't want to add to their grief. Seven years later, in January 1951, the Machettes received a communiqué from the Army. This one was unbelievable—they had Buster's body in a warehouse in England. Would they like it returned to the United States for reburial, or did they want it reinterred in France? The cruel heartache of having to relive their tragedy! His parents requested that Buster's remains be brought home, but doubt grew in his sister Florence's mind—whose body was it? How could it be Buster's if there had been no grave or knowledge of him in St. Lô, where he was reportedly buried? The answer came in January 1999, fifty-four years later, when Buster's deceased personnel file was received from the Department of the Army. The four soldiers of the 102nd killed on August 25 were not buried in St. Lô but in a civilian cemetery in Lieusaint, several miles from

Corbeil. Buster was buried as an unknown; the grave was marked only as X-40. Several months after he was killed, the four bodies were reburied in the military cemetery at Solers, which is twenty-two miles southeast of Paris. It wasn't until December 1950 that the Army approved the identification of these four soldiers, and X-40 was now known to be Buster. On April 24, 1951, Gilbert J. Machette was laid to rest in Arlington National Cemetery. With his parents present, he was given a military honors service, which consists of a six-man body bearer detail, a firing party to fire a three-rifle volley, and a bugler to play taps, as well as a chaplain. The body bearers carried the flag-draped casket to the grave and held the flag over the casket while the chaplain spoke. Following the committal service the firing party was called to attention and fired a three-rifle volley. The bugler played taps, and the body bearers folded the flag, which was then presented to his parents."

Sergeant Gilbert Machette in England 1943.
Courtesy of Edward Morrows.

August 18, 1944

Dear Catherine,

Hi Sis! Everything still going along smoothly as ever. Having a good time touring the countryside. France is a very beautiful place with its rolling hills and its green fields. The people are swell and very grateful even though a lot of them lost everything they owned. Most of the towns are pretty beat up from shell fire but the morale of the town folk is high. They're glad to see the last of the Boch. People came up to us curious at first, not knowing we are Americans, and then bursting with joy they climb all over us with bottles of wine, cider and even milk. In exchange we usually give them cigarettes and chocolate for the kids and we all feel like we're really doing our share. It's sure a swell feeling.

Enclosed is a couple of bills, one French and one Belgian, which I took from a Jerry. By the way this notebook paper I'm using was also taken from a German Sgt.

Mother writes as usual, three and four letters a day. Yesterday I received twenty-four. It's sure good to know everything's alright at home.

I'll bet you had a really swell time the week you spent at home. I sure hope the next time you get a week off I'll be able to pick you up in that new car I'm buying. How about it?

Don't worry about me. I'm taking good care of myself, and know with your help I'll come safely home. So don't worry about my keeping up my chin. It's way up and no jerry is going to keep me away from the sweet family that's waiting for me. I know God will guide me on.

Well Sis I better sign off before I run out of words. Take good care of yourself and try to keep Mom in the best of spirits.

So long for now, with all my love,

Your little brother,

Bus

. . .

Athol Nagle served with the Australian Imperial Force (AIF) during the war. His daughter, Atholene Gunn of Cremorne, New South Wales, Australia, contributed the following letter, which was written to her aunt, Nagle's sister. Ms. Gunn says that her father was the first man of the AIF in Malaya to give his life on the field of battle. He was shot in the neck by the Japanese at Gemas on January 14, 1942. Atholene was not born until April, so she never met her father.

[Excerpt]

NX47951
Sjt. Nagle A.G.
"B" Co.
2/30th Battalion
Australian Imperial Force

Malaya
18/11/41

Dear Maggie,

. . . Having unburdened my sentiment, I shall proceed to cheerier topics, for remembering Eila Wheeler Wilcot's words, "The dull old Earth must borrow its mirth, It has troubles enough of its own." Since my last letter we have had a change of scenery and camps. This camp is very new; as a matter of fact, it was in a state of incompletion when we arrived. It is constructed in the same principle as our first one, being ideally situated in a rubber estate at the foot of a ring of densely clothed hills and on the very edge of a town of considerable size and interest. The only drawback is the lack of electricity, one of the amenities of civilisation we enjoyed in our first camp. Still we are fortunate in other respects. The climate here is not nearly as trying as formerly. The air is fresher; cooler breezes spring up about 2 o'clock in the afternoon, and as we are at present in the grip of the monsoonal influence which grips this portion of the country, it rains with monotonous regularity every afternoon and night—mostly in the form of heavy soaking storms. These have the effect of enabling one to sleep at night minus that bath of perspiration which was once the order of the day and night too.

Being the first Australian troops to ever camp near this town, we naturally evoked considerable interest in the inhabitants who are mainly Chinese, Malayans, Indians and a handful of Europeans. The town is well laid out with broad streets, electrically lighted, bitumen paved and well drained. The buildings generally show an absence of filth and smells as seen and smelt in Singapore, and the Chinese Chamber of Commerce, Fire Station, Ambulance Corps building, Police Station and Barracks and the Chinese Club would do justice to any city in Australia. Of particular interest to me when we arrived here was the Mohammedan Mosque, situated just across the padang (open green playing fields containing Soccer, Rugby, hockey and cricket ovals) from our camp. It was the time of the Fast of Ramadan, when every Malayan (they are followers of Mahomet) was fasting each day from 7 o'clock in the morning until 10 at night, during which time he neither ate nor swallowed anything, not even his saliva, and periodically five times per day the "Belal" or chief priest ascended the tower and going in turn to a window facing the four main points of direction made that peculiar yodelling sound which was the call of the faithful to prayer. At night they gathered in the Mosque and for hours prayed in loud tones and in kneeling, squatting and standing positions. This continued for one lunar month, culminating upon the appearance of the new moon in "Hari Raya Puasa" (The Feast of the Fast), when all Mohammedans bedecked themselves in their brightest and gayest clothes and made merry for five days. I was fortunate enough to be a member of a party which was the guests of the local Police Club at a celebration by the Malayans on the first night of the feast.

A few weeks ago I had the good fortune to spend the day at Malacca, the cradle of European civilisation in Malaya, for it was there in 1511 that the renowned and famous Duke D'Alburquerque (pronounced Alberkirk) of Portugal ordered his men to "salute the city with artillery" from his ships lined up off shore and finally subdued the then Sultan of Malacca and took control. During the Duke's regime forts, school and churches were built and today you may, as I did, walk through the Old Fort Gate (1511), the Fort of St John (1588), the Church of St Paul's (1511), famous for its tomb of that remarkable man St Francis Xavier, who at one time was buried there, its tombstones centuries old. All these places are now ruins, but to me intensely interesting. Then wander through what must be the oldest European building in this land, for since 1511 it has been a Portuguese fort, Dutch fort, British garrison rooms and now houses the Malacca Historical Museum, the Y.M.C.A. rooms and the Government administrative offices; for Malacca has in turn been ruled by Malaya Sultans, Portuguese dons, Dutch traders and British settlers. By the time we have finished here, I'll have sufficient data and ideas to attempt to write a book on my experiences as a tourist soldier in Malaya.

A feature which has struck me rather forcibly is the "education-mindedness" of the people in general in these parts. There are schools everywhere—government, private, kindergarten, primary and high. In this town in close proximity to our Camp is the Government English School under the control of the State Council and supervised by a European Head who is changed every three years. By pure coincidence the present Head, a Mr Foster, whose term expires at the end of this year, is going to spend a portion of his leave with my cousins at Bondi. They (my cousins) were at one time in this part of the globe, principally Penang. I have not yet met the aforesaid Mr Foster, but have discovered the above facts, so am most anxious to contact him, for I would very much like to see over the school in working hours.

The Government Schools in this State are exclusively for Malayans to whom education is free. If there be any spare accommodation after the

Malayans are catered for, a few non-Malayans are taken in at fees. Consequently the Chinese have established schools of their own and the other private schools are attended principally by Chinese and Indians.

When we first arrived here there was a "rush" amongst the lads to learn the Malayan language, so we used to take night lessons at one of the private schools, but now the urge has passed and the lessons petered out. The Head was very interested in Australia and Australian educational methods, so last Saturday night he arranged for Cpt. Stoner and myself to address the elder boys and the staff—nine teachers in all. I spoke on Public School organisation and administration in New South Wales and Stoner on Australia's principal secondary industries. Judging from the acclamation supporting the chairman's vote of thanks and their desire to have us speak again at a near future date, they found the talks interesting and instructive. Then we were entertained by the male members of the Staff to a local dish called Chicken Mee, consisting of chicken, pork, shredded rice, beans, a type of spinach and chillies, all very finely cut up and eaten with fork and spoon; fruit, cigarettes and a drop of liquid cheer completed the menu. They certainly "turn on" the hospitality, these chaps, and at the same time apologising for the paucity of their efforts whilst one, as a guest, partakes of everything to an uncomfortable degree of fulness.

Well, Maggie, it appears that all too suddenly I have reached the number of pages allowed by our all-too-exacting postal service, so I shall reluctantly be compelled to draw to a conclusion, but shall write more at a later date, so for the present cheerio and love to yourself, Jack and the family, from yours ever anxiously awaiting the reply to this,

Athol

• • •

Cpl. Robert Lieberman served with the U.S. Army 104th "Timberwolf"
Infantry Division in the European theater of operations during the war. He
now lives in Alabama.

*Corporal Robert Lieberman. Courtesy of Robert
Lieberman.*

104th Timberwolf Infantry Division somewhere in Germany

January 25, 1945

I received 2 pkgs. & 2 letters. I'm glad you got a letter from me later
than the 18th already. You can lay off the socks and soap since you sent
enuf for quite a long time now.

Some people back home just don't realize the actual devastation that
is wrought on many towns in Europe. I've seen towns without one
building untouched; not merely roofs blown off but literally blown
down. Perhaps there would be enuf loose bricks to rebuild a couple of
the houses. Civilization ceases to exist for some time after the fighting;
the town being inhabited by some lone, shrapnel-riddled cow roaming

thru the wreckage for food. The stench & smell of decayed livestock is everywhere. Here and there are duds, grim reminders of what hit the town. We can always tell what houses are hit by 500 lb bombs from airplanes. A hole in the ground with wreckage strewn around is the only epitaph for the house.

We had a visit from an old member of our section who is in another one now. I think you heard about him in my letters from Carson— Harry Frampton. He made up a couple of nice songs which are terrific. I hope he wins a war bond with one.

I haven't lost one bit of my love for chemistry & I sure intend to start on it again when I hit the good old USA.

I'm trying not to get over optimistic about this Russian drive. I'm not looking for a finish at this time altho I'm keeping my fingers crossed.

Yep, a little life of this sort would sure give Betty a different slant on life!

I'm going to write a letter to Zadi tonite so I'll close with love to all.

Your loving son,

Bob

. . .

Lt. Walter Best served in the German Wehrmacht in an antitank unit, Panzer-Jaeger-Abteilung 295. For additional biographical information about Lt. Walter Best, please see Part III: Patriotism and Leadership. The following letter was written from Poland.

April 30, 1941

My darling,

Now I am sitting here in Poland. I never expected life here to be extremely pleasant; however, it is even worse than the greatest pessimist can imagine. But I'll tell you something about the journey first.

On Saturday my dream to meet my darling once again was scattered into pieces. If I had been alone on my way, I would have visited you for two days as I did before. But if you go crooked ways with your corporals, you lose your authority, and next time this will be to your own prejudice. In spite of this, I often considered visiting you. You can imagine that under these circumstances it grieved me twice as much not to travel to you.

My impressions of Warsaw first: We arrived there Monday morning at 6 a.m. It rained, which made the city look even uglier than it actually does. A dirty city and dirty people. At 8 a.m. I went to Headquarters and was told to be back at 1 p.m., because they had no information themselves so far. So we had time to stroll through the city. And as it continued raining, we visited a café. I ordered a cup of coffee and two pieces of cake. The price of the cake was 30 Pf. per piece and a cup of coffee was 70 Pf. I thought to myself: Alright—really good coffee—you may pay much more than usual for this. It turned out to be only malt coffee, however, and the pieces of cake were even smaller than a matchbox.

Like the coffee, everything is twice as expensive here as in Germany. There are no ration tickets here, and you can buy everything. But nobody can pay for it.

At noon they gave me orders to go to Krakow. After seeing a film, we left at 8 p.m. and arrived at 7 a.m. the next morning. At 11 a.m. we went on to Debica and from there to Terziana. There we found our detachment. The mud on the streets stretched far beyond our ankles. The commanding officer took me to my company in his car, for he had not yet been there and wanted to have a look at the quarters. The corporals followed walking.

The little village, in which my company took up quarters, is called Darana. On the way the car got stuck, and it took four hours of labor to move it out of the mud. The commanding officer and I walked meanwhile, maybe two kilometers, which lasted one hour. You cannot imagine all this dirt and mud. Our company has fairly good quarters, but our vehicles stand in the mud up to their axles.

And now, let me tell you about my room: It is in one of the best houses here, made of wood with a thatched roof. Inside there is a kitchen and one room. The inhabitants have to sleep in the kitchen and in the stable. I sleep in the living-room. It is large and whitewashed. The furniture is a table, two chairs, a bed and 4,000 images of the Virgin Mary. There is another table in the kitchen with two chairs. I ordered my men to clean the table, the chairs and the floor. They provided for the bed and a new layer of straw, too. Fortunately I have one of my sleeping bags with me, and my attendant even brought a comforter of silk. He did not even forget a table cover. The furniture is completed by a small oven and a carbide lamp. So I feel at home somehow. Since I put your picture on my table, I am in my familiar "war home" again.

Fortunately the people keep their house clean. But in front of the house the dirt is knee-deep. The Polish have a simple way to solve the problem. They walk barefooted, even when it is very cold. By the house there is a bucket filled with water to wash your feet before entering the house. But you will find this achievement of civilization only in few cases, particularly in houses with a wooden floor. And there are only three of this kind in the village. The others have a clay soil, and so you don't have to wash your feet.

Now, my darling, I think you can imagine how we are here. But all this will be over one day, maybe very soon. Tomorrow I'll tell about a reconnaissance mission I had today—or more correctly experienced today.

My very best regards and a long kiss,
your Walter

How is your mother? Regards to her.

• • •

T/4 Sgt. Clarence McIlrath served with the 301st Ordnance Heavy Maintenance Company, which was attached to the Fifteenth U.S. Army. Sergeant McIlrath's grandmother was born in Germany, and, according to his daughter, Darlene Blasing of Ohio, who contributed his letter, he "had doubts about the negative press the Germans received, especially after finding the churches in Germany intact and functioning. Undoubtedly, he was also trying to calm any fears his wife may have had by speaking of the beauty of the churches and the friendliness of the people he met."

The 301st had arrived in England on February 16, 1945, and crossed the Channel to Le Havre, France, on March 4 and 5. They remained in a camp near St. Valerie—a "tent city" called Camp Lucky Strike—until April 5, when they were designated to be a unit of the Fifteenth U.S. Army, Lieutenant General Gerow commanding. They left Camp Lucky Strike on April 5 and arrived in Herzogenrath, Germany, near the country's western border, the following day. There they were billeted in an abandoned button factory. Thus, they were able to go to Belgium and Holland during their free time.

Sergeant Clarence McIlrath with wife, Irene, who was visiting him in South Carolina before he was sent overseas. Courtesy of Darlene M. Blasing.

April 15, 1945
Germany

Dear Honey,

How are my darlings today? It has been nice here today. I went to eleven o'clock Mass this morning in a German Catholic church. It was really beautiful. A lot of the stuff we heard about the German's attitude toward religion was a lot of propaganda, I believe, because you still see Priests and Nuns around here and this church we went to wasn't damaged hardly at all and all of the furnishings were in good shape in the church. The priest even wore German vestments. We were in a Catholic church in Holland this afternoon. It was nice too. All of the homes around here that I've seen have crucifixes in them and almost all of the pictures they have are Holy pictures.

The Holland people seem awfully nice. They are all friendly. It keeps you busy saying hello when you walk down the street. The children come up and say hello and then they will take a hold of your hand and walk along with you. Most of the younger folks can speak pretty good English. They teach it to them in school. The children are all neat and clean. They ask you for candy (for themselves), and cigarettes for papa.

The Holland people were harder hit than the Belgians. The Belgians have quite a few cars and plenty to eat where the Dutch don't have any too much to eat, and I didn't see a civilian car where I was today.

I noticed one thing today that seemed funny. There were quite a few young kids in beer gardens, not that the beer would hurt them any though. A kid could drink, any beer that I've had yet, all day long and not feel it.

I want to pick up some souvenirs for you in Belgium when I go in Tuesday if I can. I'll send you some Belgian money too. We'll have to save this foreign money for Chucky, when he gets a little older.

We got quite a bit of mail today. I didn't get any, but it should start coming through good again. Every time we move it takes a little time for it to catch up. We are lucky compared to some of the boys up toward the front. I know one fellow that didn't get any mail for six weeks. What have you decided to do with the car? Ma said you wanted to keep it. Do whatever you want to with it, honey, but it is worth less all of the time.

I guess I'd better close for now, darling, and write Ma a few lines. Goodnight, darling. Lots of hugs and kisses for my darlings.

Your loving husband,
Clarence

• • •

Keith Laidler served in the Royal Australian Air Force. He died in action when his plane was shot down on the way back to England after a raid on Germany in August 1944. He was twenty-two years old at the time. Craig K. Curtis of Geelong, Victoria, Australia, contributed the following letter home in which his cousin describes his travels in the United States.

Aus 430373
Sgt. Laidler, G.J.K.,
Aus. P.O. R.A.A.F.,
Kodak House
London, England

13th January, 1944

Dear All,

Just a few lines to let you know that I am all right and hope that all of you at home are the same. Today I met Don Hassett and will soon be going home. Well, here goes to give you an idea of my trip since I left

Australia. After leaving Australia we arrived in America and after seeing San Francisco we began our travel by Pullman train across America. Four of us had a small compartment to ourselves and the negro porter used to make our beds for us. The fortnight on the train which is centrally heated we saw snow covered mountains which looked beautiful in the moonlight. Ogden was the first big town that we stopped at—this is after the Great Salt Lake which is 15 miles by 30 miles and 20 feet deep. Next we saw Denver and we went for a walk into the town. I am sending home some photos of this town. Next came Kansas City and Chicago. A snow fight at Kansas was quite good. The meals on the train were very good and at some towns [where] we stopped the local people came to the train with coffee and cakes. Then after a few more days we arrived in New York. We left for an Army camp and next day we started leave in New York. To begin with I was impressed with the tall buildings. The first place we went to was the Anzac Club where they gave us the best places to stay at and on this leave I stayed at the Knickerbocker Hotel. In the daytime I travelled around and saw Radio City which occupies a whole block and also the Music Hall which seats 6,000 people. Also saw the only theatre that has an ice show on the stage; it was "Stars on Ice." Also I saw the Empire State Building which has 102 stories and stands 1,250 feet. I went up to the top and I saw the most amazing sights I have ever seen. There is hardly any petrol ration in America and there are 10,000 taxis in New York alone. Also I visited the Central Park and the zoo which is quite small compared to Melbourne's or Sydney's zoo. The cars they have are most modern compared to ours and nearly everyone in America seems to have a car even if they don't own a house. In the second leave in New York I stayed at the Century Hotel. We were in New York for Christmas Day and a chap from the Anzac Club took Don Ford and myself out for Christmas dinner which by the way was an eight-course meal. New York never seems to sleep as the shops don't close till near midnight and the theatres at 3 o'clock. So you can see that when we went out to see the shows in the night we wouldn't get home very early. Sunday is late also except that the main shops are closed. At the theatres you would see a film followed by a stage show which had different well-known personalities as Tommy Dorsey and his orchestra, Kathryn Grayson and Rags Ragland, both M.G.M. film stars. How is dad's arm getting along and how did Joyce do in her exams? Answer all letters by sending airgraph as they are faster—see post office about forms. This is the third letter I have written but it may get home first as others we posted ordinary, not even air mail. I got plenty of cigarettes in America. I enjoyed myself everywhere so far as you can see I am enjoying it. Don't forget any Scottish addresses of Uncle Andy's relatives or the Christies. I will write shortly to Ron. I met Max Potter and Max Leversha is on leave. Well, I have run short; don't forget to pass this letter around to all friends and give them my best wishes for the next year and same to you.

I remain,

Your loving son,

Keith

. . .

Sgt. Charles William Owen Erwood volunteered for the New Zealand Artillery soon after the outbreak of war in September 1939, when he was eighteen-years-old, and he served with Number 1504, B Troop, Twenty-fifth Battery, Fourth Field Regiment, New Zealand Artillery, Second New Zealand Expeditionary Force. His niece, Sally Erwood-Carryer of Morley, Western Australia, who submitted the following letter, says that, like a majority of his fellow soldiers, he had never been overseas before and that when the First Echelon of the New Zealand troops arrived in Egypt in January 1940, the contrast with their home country was striking. In the following letters, written by then-bombardier Erwood to his sister, he describes his experiences in Egypt after being there for six weeks. After surviving the disastrous Greek and Cretan campaigns in early 1941, he died on November 30 of wounds sustained while fighting against the German army in the western desert.

*Sergeant Charles William Owen Erwood during his
final embarkation leave in December 1939 when
he had just turned nineteen-years-old. Courtesy of
Sally Erwood-Carryer.*

Egypt
No. 1504
Bdr. C.W. O Erwood
B Troop
25th Bty, NZFA
2nd NZEF
c/o G.P.O.
Wellington
29.3.40

My darling Val,

I'm afraid I have to make the usual belated apology for not writing
sooner, but I hope you will forgive me. I don't know why it is, but I find

it (or have found it) frightfully difficult to settle down to writing. I am seeing so many new and different things, and forming so many new impressions that I have found it hard to write about them. However I have settled down pretty thoroughly now, and I hope to be able to write weekly from now on. Don't be disappointed if the mails are irregular though, Val, as of course the whole service as far as mail boats are concerned is not running to schedule.

As I have explained to Mother, the letter which I have written her is really to you both, as I know you will not expect me to write about the trip again. [The voyage on the troopship *Empress of Canada*, from Wellington to Egypt via Fremantle, Western Australia, and Colombo, Ceylon.]

Well, I hope you received my cable alright, Val. [For her eighteenth birthday on March 19, 1940.] I will be sending you a present as soon as I find a suitable one. There is so much trash to be bought here in Cairo at such inviting prices, that one has to be extremely discriminating. Buying an article in most shops in Cairo is extremely different and much more difficult than procuring the same article in Hamilton [New Zealand, where his family was living]. One enters a shop here, clutching a few piastres in one's extremely light pocket, and while mentally figuring out the price one intends paying, keeps a sharp eye on the villain behind the counter. To call him a villain is to flatter him. In a falsely optimistic tone one inquires whether he has the desired article. Why of course he has it, sare, the finest example of its kind in Cairo. So far so good. The thing is produced and its virtues extolled to the high heavens. One almost hates to bring him down to earth by any sordid mention of money, but the thing must be done.

In as casual and firm a tone as one can muster one pops the question. How much? He eyes one sadly as though he hates to part with the damned thing at any price, then shrugs his shoulders and says casually, "to you, sare, only fifty piastres." One's heart turns over at the thought of the twenty piastres one grips. However, he does not expect to be paid the fifty (his optimism has waned a little in the few weeks we have been here), and one certainly has no intention of paying it. There are various methods of beating the crook down. There is one school of thought which advises straight out haggling. This is too strenuous and is often not worth the effort. An alternative method is to examine the article scornfully, deride its quality, its value, the shopkeeper's honesty, in fact to work oneself up into believing that the thing is worthless. This is rather a dangerous method as it causes ill will and sometimes violence. The method which I both advocate and practice with a certain amount of success, is the light laugh and the attitude of "Well of course it's a marvelous piece of work and well worth the money, but I must try some place else." This invariably produces the desired effect and has the added attraction of placing us both on an amicable footing. From there it is a short step to procuring the thing at maybe five piastres more than I intended paying and leaving the place in mutual goodwill. The whole business was exasperating to us at first but now we treat it as a matter of course. Naturally there are some shops where articles are listed at a certain price and no amount of haggling in the world will reduce that price. They are the shops for poor soldiers to avoid. They are simply receptacles for a soldier's pay.

Well, I haven't replied to your letters yet, Val, so I had better do so now.

Yes, I did get rather a shock when I saw that you were back at the old place. However I suppose you are away from it by now. Here's hoping so anyway. I see that Din has taken the plunge. His leavetaking was typical of the old reprobate, wasn't it! I'm looking forward to seeing him again. Incidentally I shall probably be seeing your late friend Mac in the near future. Re the latter. He is quite a decent chap in his own way, but he is definitely not the sort of chap for [a] kid like you. Leave his sort alone and concentrate on the just-left-high-school type. You won't have any heart trouble then. However you'll learn sometime apropos of all this. You have mentioned a Brian a good deal in your letters but you have omitted to mention his surname, his unit and his rank. Without that information my dear, I am afraid I haven't the faintest chance of tracing him. Give those particulars and I'll look him up, Val.

7th April 1940

I'm afraid I've left this letter a bit longer, dear, but I haven't been able to settle down to writing this past week.

Well I have just got your letter dated the 25.2.40 so I will answer it right away. Taking your questions and remarks in order.

No, I have definitely not been out with Gippo (Egyptian) lassies. I'm surprised at that remark coming from you. You know I'm not a boy like that.

Yes I do think the photo you took of Mother is wonderful. It's the most treasured thing I have. I'd like a good one of you too, Val.

I suppose Alec Hayes has a good reason for not joining up. It doesn't do to condemn a man without being fully aware of all circumstances, you know.

You must have been disappointed at not being able to see the "Achilles" come into port. As a matter of fact, I am one up on you there, as I actually did see her come in and the march through Auckland. On a newsreel of course.

No I didn't force my way into any photos at the embarkation. I was too busy trying to see a face I knew on the wharf. I didn't see one.

The flies may be bad at Hamilton, but you made a very foolish remark, my girl, when you said they must be as bad as they are here. In Egypt the flies and the sand are always with us. In great quantities!

That was a typical action for Malcolm St. Clair, don't you think?

Now to the cream of your questions. You ask if I have swum in the Nile. Let me just say that anyone who has the horrible misfortune to fall into the Nile is immediately innoculated. Is it necessary for me to say more? No! We have an excellent swimming pool here, good hot and cold showers and plenty of fresh water. It is not at all necessary for us to go within co-ee of the Nile, and we don't.

No, I didn't see you kiss Monty good-bye but I'm quite sure he enjoyed it.

Righto, that is all I think.

I am trying to think of something interesting and noteworthy to tell you about this place. Perhaps I had better tell you what I can about the camp. It is similar to Hopu Hopu [the camp near Hamilton, New Zealand, where he did his training] except that they have a really good canteen (incidentally Bombardiers have a canteen of their own) and an exceptionally good cinema with a different picture every night. Not second-class stuff either. You think of any first-class picture which has been to Hamilton and nine times out of ten it will either have been shown here or will be coming. Added to that we have shows on at half-time which are worth pounds to see, and all for the glorious sum of 3 piastres to 5 piastres which works out at about 7½d to 1/-(seven pence halfpenny to one shilling). Incidentally you may be interested to know that one pound sterling is worth 100 piastres, which makes 1 piastre worth about 2½d! (two pence halfpenny). It is easy to confuse piastres with pennies, which is rather an expensive practice as you can imagine. The only other essential difference as compared with Nga [Ngaru-awhia, where the Hopu Hopu camp was located] is that instead of grass we spend our time walking on dusty sand. Still we are pretty well used to it now.

There are quite a number of good-looking girls about Cairo and Maadi. Every nationality is gathered here and it is rather strange to hear a foreign language issuing from the face of a beautiful girl who looks as though she should speak nothing but English and doesn't know a word of it. It makes things rather difficult at times. I have found that I have had to trot out my French quite often and brush it up a little. I shudder to think what I may have said quite innocently at times. L'importe!

Well my darling, I will tell you a lot more in my next letter but I must get this away now.

Your loving brother,
Owen

P.S. I was frightfully pleased to have those few lines from that illustrious band of so-called workers, with whom you associate. Please convey to them my heartfelt gratitude for their charity.

Extra Special for Roma

Heartiest congratulations, you great big beautiful doll. You might have waited for me though.

Not So Special for Ada

No, a question mark was not necessary. If a girl is going to send me her love, I refuse to have any conditions attached to it. Here's mine anyway, Ada!

Quite Special for Ros

Your touching hopes for my material comfort were most pleasing, Ros. That crack about the mummies was uncalled for, I think. What!

Special for Alec

I sympathise with you, Alec. I think it's time you rid yourself of that pestilent female horde and came over to our side. Thanks for the note. Hope to see some of the battery soon. [The Second Medium Battery of the Territorial Army that both men served in before the war.]

Owen

PART VI

POWs—Life in the Camps

Airman Jim Cahir served with the Royal Air Force Bomber Command of the 466th Squad, flying a four-engine Halifax heavy bomber in 1943. After being shot down and spending eighteen months as a prisoner of war in Germany, he was sent to a hospital in Halifax, England, where he wrote this letter. He now lives in Melbourne, Victoria, Australia. He submitted this letter in memory of his pilot, Flight Sergeant Patrick Edwards of the Royal Australian Airforce Squadron 466, to whom he owes his life.

W/o Fs. Cahir
Aus. 419441
Kodak House
London
May 20th 45

Dear Mum, Pat & Vincent,

    Well, here I am in England once again. You have no idea how wonderful it feels to be a free man, just to look out of the window and not see barbed wire with machine gun forts along it is a pleasure in itself. Once again I feel like an individual instead of just an animal ordered around by the fear of a gun—it's a marvelous feeling to be free!

Well, I don't know where to begin the story; I think the best plan would be to go back to [the] night of Dec 20th 1943. We were attacked by German aircraft just after bombing Frankfurt on Main; the fighters set us on fire and the kite went into a dive for 10,000 feet before Pat managed to pull it out; he then ordered us to bail out and I think we were at a height of approx. 8,000 ft when I jumped.

I landed without injury and did the usual things such as hiding my chute etc. I was eventually picked up twenty-four hours later by a German who handed me over to the Gestapo who in turn gave us over to the Luftwaffe and whence my life behind the wire began. Well then looking back over that night I have no one else on this earth to thank for saving my life but my "Skipper" Pat Edwards; it was only by his bravery that I got out with the rest of the crew. After we had been hit Pat remained very calm, fought the controls and eventually pulled the kite out of a death dive for just long enough to get his crew out, his last words to us still ring in my ears: "Good luck boys and if those so and so's catch you don't tell them anything." When I was taken to the Luftwaffe HQ's I was told that the rest of my crew had died; it appears that they tell everybody this to try & break their nerves which don't require much breaking at that stage of the game. I then spent six days in solitary confinement on bread & watery soup whilst they tried to get information out of me. Christmas Day 1943 was the worst day of my life. I think I was just beginning to feel the shock of the crash, I was in solitary confinement, I didn't know who of the crew was dead or alive, and I kept thinking of you at home worrying over me. I am sure I nearly went crazy that day, I wanted to laugh, cry, and shout all at once; when I think of it even now I shiver!

Boxing Day I was taken out of my cell & the following day I met George Rhett & the rest of the boys & we departed from Frankfurt by train to Muhlberg where I remained until I was liberated by the Russians. I was never at Luft 3, but our mail and parcels were supposed to come through that camp.

Stalag 1VB. was an army camp but there was about 1,200 RAF chaps there; the rest of the camp consisted of Americans, French, Dutch, Italians, Russians, Danes, in fact every nationality in Europe; on the day of liberation there were 27,000 prisoners in the camp.

We lived in huts, 90 feet long, usually 220 men to a hut but on occasions we have had over 400 in huts built for 200. In these huts we lived, cooked, smoked, talked and slept. Our beds consisted of three-tier bunks reaching to the roof; in bad times we had to sleep two to a bed or on a brick floor which used to freeze in winter. Jan. 45 is a month I will never forget in my life because of the shortage of food, fuel & blankets; it's a wonder more chaps didn't die. The health of a lot of chaps broke down and in the winter of 43–44 typhus broke out, which earned the death of hundreds of nationals other than British; the chap in the bed beside me caught typhus but recovered from it. The barrack rooms were full of fleas and the Germans used to [do] nothing about it.

The food situation was very serious; I can honestly say that the Red Cross kept us alive; the food the Germans used [to] give us I would not give to any decently bred dog. Please don't think me bitter toward Germans; I don't think I am! All I am doing is looking back on things & giving you my own opinion.

Since being back in England I have thought a great deal over the last eighteen months and I have changed a lot in my outlook. When I landed in Germany I was pretty green & young in outlook even though I kidded myself I was a man of the world and perhaps I even acted as one; it was not until I got behind the barbed wire did I see what war did to men.

Men who had been living peaceful lives suddenly whipped away from their families thrown into a dirty camp and forced to work on hardly enough food to live on. Then shot dead because they were hungry and stole potato peelings from a rubbish cart; another man shot dead because he was hungry and attempted to steal some strawberries from a German garden.

When I first went to IVB it used to make me sick to see Russians grovelling in the dirt looking for something to eat, [illegible] that had been lying on the ground for weeks, fighting & kicking one another over a piece of spud peeling, but after a few weeks I became like the rest of the camp a silent spectator knowing that one day the tables would be turned.

Jerry's prison was composed of men, women & children. Do you remember Warsaw? Well in our camp there were 1,000 women & 600 children between the ages of 6 and 10 years who were deported from Warsaw and were destined to work for Hitler & his allies; that is only one case of forced labour; there were thousands of young girls & women in Germany like the one I met who had been taken from their houses in occupied territory, tattooed with a number on their arm & put to work. Well, Mum, if I don't stop this you will think I have become a cynic and developed a hatred of the Germans, I assure you nothing of the kind has happened; as far as I am concerned I neither like nor hate the Germans and I think they deserve everything that's coming to them.

Now to get back to the camp; we were liberated by the Russians on app. the 23rd, the day that they linked up with the Americans at a place called [illegible]. It was quite an exciting week for us; as you no doubt know we were hemmed in on all sides and the SS put up quite some resistance; air activity preceding the liberation was great; the American fighter pilots used to put on shows for us over the camp, but the [illegible] was obtained when fighters stopped an ammo train about ½ mile from the camp; did that train go up with a bang!

The night before the Russians arrived the German guards packed up & [illegible] for their lives and it was not until the morning after we went out on parade to be counted that we discovered that we owned the camp. The Russians left us in the camp & continued their mopping up operations. About a week later they told us we had to get out as they needed the camp, so we went to a place called [illegible] about 20 km's away and installed ourselves in a German Military Barracks; myself & nine other chaps thought we would like a little comfort for once so we lived in a flat that had been occupied by a Nazi official. We spent about a week here in [illegible] until we got a bit tired of it; then we decided that the Russians were not doing much about getting us home, so we walked out on them and hiked along the road until we reached the Mulda River at a place called [illegible]. There the Yanks picked us up & fed us like kings.

We then traveled to Halle, spent a few days there and eventually were flown out by Dakotas to Brussels where Danes picked us up to fly us to England.

On reaching England I was admitted to hospital suffering from malnutrition. I feel O.K. but the old tummy can't get used to good meals; consequently I am on a milk diet; I expect to be in hospital two to three weeks so don't worry over me.

I have lost a bit weight, but on a milk diet it shouldn't be long before I put it on again. When I think of all the girls at home doing all kinds of things to get their weight down I smile; tell them to send a stamped addressed envelope to me & I will [send] back the secret to them.

The rest of IVB is still at [illegible]; the way the Russians are carrying on they could be there for months. The Russians are a funny crowd! I still can't figure them out so I won't attempt to give you my opinion of them in a letter.

I had a visit from Auntie Agnes & Uncle Shamus yesterday; I think they expected me to be nothing but skin & bones; I began to feel sorry I had disappointed them. They brought with them a couple of your letters, also a few from Mary; they also told me that Vincent had joined the Navy; nice going, Vincent! I hope you enjoy the life. Don't worry over him, Mum; this war will be over very shortly & we will all be back with you.

I am enclosing a list of letters I received from you; I received many other letters from other people and answered them all in one way or the other whilst I was in Germany. I will write to everybody again within the next couple of weeks. At the moment I am a bit out of practice writing letters, and besides it's not the easiest job whilst in bed. You might tell anybody that has written to me that I really appreciate their kindness and I will drop them a line later on.

I don't think there is anything you can send me. I am expecting RAAF HQ's down here within the next couple of days; they ought to be able to enlighten me on certain things. Yes, there is one thing you can send me—that is a "fruit cake." It's a few months since I tasted a good one.

Well, Mum, I must close. I know I have left a lot out and I will save it until I get home. This letter writing is not such an easy job [as] I thought it to be or perhaps it's just because I am out of practice. Kindest regards to everybody back home.

Love XXXX

Jim

• • •

Radio Officer Odd Conrad Holm served with the Norwegian Merchant Marines. He sailed many dangerous Atlantic convoy crossings, before his ship was taken by Germans. He was a prisoner of war in Morocco and Algeria in 1941 and 1942, spending time in nine prison camps. The following letter was translated and contributed by his daughter, Siri Lawson, who was born in Norway and now lives in Oklahoma.

Glasgow
Aug. 25–1945

Dear Mom,

Today I've finally had the pleasure of hearing from you. The last letter I received from you was dated Sept. 1942; in other words almost 3 years ago. The postal services have not been quite normal these past few years; besides there wasn't much to tell. I also have the impression that you all thought I was in Tangier in '41–'42 and the beginning of '43. Granted, I've been in various places since I left home in a snowstorm in

1937, but never in Tangier. Therefore, I'll briefly try to tell you where I've been since April of 1940.

In the early days of April we were on board S/S *Ringulv* in Swansea, England, loading coal for Norway. We were then assembled in a convoy consisting of about fifty ships and headed for Norway. On April 9* I was in the lookout barrel on the front mast of the *Ringulv* looking for land and humming "No ser eg atter slike fjell og daler"†, but that turned out to be a lie! Instead I saw some German bombers which had their own way of welcoming us home. After they had dropped their bombs all of the German planes were shot down by the British fighter planes that were escorting us. After several attacks the entire convoy returned to England. Later we went to Havre in France and unloaded the coal. We stayed there for about a month until the Germans chased us out. Havre was not very peaceful in those days. We were bombed day and night. We then left Havre with 1,500 refugees on board. The youngest was a week old and the oldest had no idea how old he was. It was, by the way, doubtful that any of us would grow much older. Several of the refugees lost their minds during the trip. We as a crew worked 24 hrs. a day until we put the refugees ashore on the west coast of France, whereupon we continued to Bordeaux. The Germans went by land while we went by sea. We arrived in Bordeaux at about the same time. Then the same circus started. After a while we had to go on and continued to Casablanca in North Africa. That meant "the evening and the latch on the door"‡ as far as sailing for the time being. With the help of French Nazis the Germans took control of all of North Africa. I was finally able to get in touch with you through an address in Tangier. The letters were smuggled across the border to Tangier. If the Germans had known what was going on, who knows what the consequences would have been.

The crew of the *Ringulv* was the first to be placed in concentration

---

*the day of the German invasion of Norway.
†Norwegian song line meaning "Again I see my mountains and valleys."
‡Old Norwegian expression meaning "lock up for the night and go to bed" or "call it a night."

camps.* We were in 8 different ones in the course of nineteen months. Three of my shipmates died during that time. In one of the camps I fortunately came down with diptheria and was admitted to something which vaguely resembled a hospital. So I was in good shape, and was content with life and my existence, and without that there's no point in living, as "Broom-Lars" used to say. In one of the other camps I came down with malaria. Was very sick for a while, was treated but lost a lot of weight. If Karl Dala had been there he probably would have asked me if I wished I were stillborn. But I got through it without lasting harm I hope.

From another camp I and two others made an attempt to escape and get across to Gibraltar. We managed to stay in hiding for about a month, but were turned in by a female who sold us some food. If one wants to form an opinion of the conditions in hell, all one has to do is confide in that devilish creature, the woman. We were consequently arrested. I remember there were forty-two of us in a cell but nineteen different nationalities. We had a grand old time and did what we could to stay there, but in the end we were returned to the camp.

In November of 1942, when the Allied forces invaded Africa, we were in a camp about 350 miles of the city Oran. It was like being up in the marshes as far as the view goes. Not a straw of grass, sand as far as the eye could see. We didn't get much food to speak of. It was not unusual to have to wait in line for hours to get a bottle of water. On the other hand we had plenty enough lice. Still, it wasn't necessary to go home to change our shirts. Naturally, we were happy when we were freed.

While we were there we were asked daily if we wanted to go home. A Trondheim guy by the name of Georg Hermannsen was very sick and went home in the summer of 1942. He sent greetings to you from me. He knew the Holm family in Rosenborg St. very well. I assume you received those greetings.

---

*Because of a mix-up, Siri Lawson says, the only crew to be placed in labor camps as opposed to regular internment camps were the crews from other Norwegian ships.

While I was in Africa I received several letters from you. You were all good at writing me, and especially Solveig, who probably wrote very often. A lot of Solveig's letters had been subjected to German censorship. It wasn't unusual to find several lines missing. But Solveig managed to fool them quite cleverly and told me almost everything of interest. It was very encouraging to receive your letters. A while back I read old letters from the lack of new ones and at the same time I counted them up. I found that half of them were from Solveig. I haven't met a single person I know since I left home so it's great to get news.

When I was done in Africa I went on board a ship called "Nyhorn." Was there for about a year. Then I attended Radio Officer's School in London for nine months.* That was very interesting. I think I did quite well. While in school I received a radiogram from you through a friend of mine.

I have now been on board here[†] for close to a year. We've been going between here and America the whole time and it has been going very well, usually in convoys consisting of a hundred ships. We left England the day before the capitulation. The day passed without incident except for a dozen depth charges. It was the escort vessels going a couple of extra rounds with the remaining German U-boats.

The last time we were in New York I wrote you a few words on a postcard which I handed to the pilot before we went out to sea. I hear you received it. It was illegal to send letters at that time. Last time we were in America I received letters from Kari and Solveig. I was almost afraid to open and read them; this was only three weeks ago so it took a long time before I heard anything from you. Just before we left America last time I was able to connect to Bergen Radio and sent you a radio letter of twenty words which I'm sure you have received by now.

---

*the Norwegian government had established schools in London for Norwegian sailors as they were in need of officers.
[†] *Thorshov*

We were supposed to start going to the Eastern countries, but it looks like that won't happen now that the Japs have been blown to bits and are finished for good.

I hear NN has gotten married in Cardiff. I was there two months ago but didn't know that at the time. There are several Norwegians who have gotten married in Norway as well as in England and America. I guess it's handy to have a few wives here and there, but it must be hard to get the budget to balance for many of these bigamists. The Norwegian women have possibly changed somewhat these past few years, but I'm sure they're still first class compared to the foreign ones. There are exceptions of course.

During the past two years I have received many letters from my cousin and her daughter in America, and also from uncle Johan. They want me to come and visit them, but I haven't gotten around to it yet. My cousin's name is Alma Wilson. She's the daughter of Markus Holm and Johan Holm's wife. Alma is 58 years old and has been a widow for many years. They live in Dell Rapids, South Dakota.

I remember when I was on the train from Stjørdal on my way to Trondheim to go on board the *Gudrid*. I wondered then if I would ever be able to make a return trip. There hasn't been much hope of that during the war. As you know a lot of explosives have been used out here the past few years. "They aimed for the eyes" as John Moan used to say. Now that the war is over and if nothing unexpected happens I may have the great pleasure of standing by the window on the train from Trondheim to Hegra. That will be quite an occasion. I don't know yet when that will be. We can't all go home; if we did the supplies to war torn countries would be affected. We are now probably going to Mexico to load oil. This will be a nice trip which will take about three weeks. We have just gotten a new radio which cost fifteen hundred kroner, so it's not junk.

I am sitting here listening to the court proceedings from the Quisling case. You don't need to be a lawyer to understand that he ought to be hung any time now. When I think about the Axial forces I have to quote the Frosta woman: "She started it herself; she ended it herself; now she has to suffer the consequences herself."

You say you are doing so well. I don't really believe that. You know "well" is quite an expandable expression. You'll have to write and tell me how things are. I have also received some letters from all of my siblings except Thora and big brother who haven't written, but the mail is so slow. I'll write them all as soon as I can. For now I'll send a copy of this letter to those I heard from first. Hope you all write again. I would like to see Stjødalens Blad.*

So I'll end this for now. I'll send you a telegram when we are in the middle of the Atlantic again. All the best then, Mom, and give my regards to family and friends.

Love,

Odd

. . .

Michael Menzies, his brother, Jack, and five companions were serving in the Ninth Brigade of the Thirty-fourth Battalion for the New Zealand Army as coast watchers in the northern Gilbert Islands when they were captured by the Japanese on December 10, 1941. Michael Menzies's son, Kevin Menzies of Auckland, New Zealand, who contributed his father's letters, says the men were behind enemy lines spying on the shipping movements of a major Japanese naval base, making them among the first Allies to make contact with the Japanese after Japan entered the war. They were taken to Zentsuji War Prison Camp on the island of Shikoku, Japan, and were probably the first captured Allies in Japan. For three years Michael Menzies did not receive any mail, but he continued to write letters to a friend of his in the Royal New Zealand Air Force, to his brother, Pat, in the Royal Air Force, and to other family members. He remained a prisoner of war until 1945.

---

*a local newspaper for the Hegra area.

*Michael Menzies. Courtesy of Kevin
Menzies.*

C/—Mrs. S Hughes 11/6/43

Dear Pat,

Please forgive me for not writing you before this. As for what you are
doing or where you are I haven't the slightest idea as I have not received
mail in any shape or form for over seventeen months during which time
Jack and I have been "Prisoners Of War" in Japan.

Naturally it's a great strain worrying and wondering how you are, but
apart from that both Jack and I are safe, well & unharmed. Don't worry
over us, Pat, as we have been fortunate enough to be together & I can
assure you that things are not so bad as they may seem to you. The
length and contents of this letter are limited so try not to be disappointed if they don't come up to your expectations.

I hope and pray that you are safe & well. Take every care of yourself,
Pat, so that you'll be in the pink of condition for our reunion in the not
too distant future.

Your loving brother,
Mick

20/6/43

All hands are directed to write a letter to be placed on file in case enquiries are made through the "Red Cross" concerning you.

If such inquiries are made this letter will be taken from the file and cabled through the "Red Cross" that as of such a date your health, etc, was ". . . . ." The letter should be addressed to anyone that might make inquiries.

Letter Form:
Prison No (365)   Date
Past and Present health.
Impression of daily life and work you do (if you desire).
Business
Signature.

(I have written this but not turned it in)
Note: a) not over 250 words

     b) Insert everything of importance that you placed in your previous letters.

During the period I have been a Prisoner of War my health has been kept in remarkably fine shape even though my diet & the climatic conditions here are somewhat reversed to what I had been accustomed to. From the heat of the tropics to the cold miserable winter months was quite a shock for my system to take, but owing to the fair treatment & interest shown towards us, serious illness was prevented. Twice I have been innoculated and vaccinated against diseases & many other quaint medical examinations I have had. At present my health is in a favourable condition with the exception of the mental strain of worrying, as I have no news from anyone for over 17 months, & the lack of entertainment.

A party of us prisoners leaves camp at 6 a.m. every day and returns at 6.45 p.m. after a heavy day's manual labour at a Railway Depot. I get one day off in six, which I spend washing clothes & catching up on some of my sleep. There are various classes every day & a concert once a week but us railway employees have been deprived of the opportunity of attending them as we are either too late in arriving back or worn out & very tired.

Sgt Menzies P. 41599
C/—New Zealand House
415 The Strand
London
England

11/4/44   250 words

Dear Pat,

Both Jack & myself have been Prisoners of War in Japan for over 2 years 5 months & during this period of time I have not received mail from New Zealand, although I have been fortunate in receiving a letter from America in which was your address, and the very pleasant information of your engagement. Congratulations Pat & Freda from both Jack & myself. I suppose you will be married by the time you receive this, so once again here's our most heartfelt & sincere congratulations for a most happy & prosperous married life. I'm just bubbling over with questions and news for you but unfortunately our mail is limited & restricted so much that I find it hard to know just what to write.

As regards to our health we are both sound in body & mind not withstanding that our existence here is not what we have been accustomed to in the past. Before I forget to tell you, my address is, Prt.

Michael Menzies, (63994), Zentsuji War Prisoners Camp, Shikoku Island, Japan. I want a nice long newsy letter from you, Pat, & possibly one from Freda too, & don't forget to enclose a photo, as all my personal effects were lost when I was "picked up."

Do you intend to return to New Zealand after the war? Have you been inspired in any way? Have you heard from New Zealand—Spence or Sally—Well, Pat, I'm forced to close now, so don't worry over Jack or me as we are together in the same Prison Camp. Have a hell of a good time, Pat, but above all take good care of yourself.

I remain your loving brother,

Mick

(Have to reduce to 150 words postcard size)

• • •

Col. Willibald Scherer served with the German forces as commander of Stalag Luft 1 from 1942 until the end of 1944. Colonel Scherer wrote the following letter to his wife, Marie Luise Scherer, and to his son, Stephan J. M. Scherer, who contributed his father's letter. He says that his father was removed from service after he was accused of being an Anglophile and didn't follow the order to separate Jewish from non-Jewish prisoners of war. Stephan J. M. Scherer lives in Fuerth Bay, Germany. Dr. Robert Larson from Florida helped translate the letter.

3/2/44 in the evening

Dearest Ise,

About the weather; yes, that was a terrible disaster. The first spring temperatures, tempting you to go outside and work in the garden, and now, after two days, this abrupt weather change!

For 24 hours the storm direction has changed from south to west and now a blizzard is shaking and howling through the area, and so we are aghast and disgusted about it. Under such circumstances, watching the

Colonel Willibald Scherer (fourth from left) in front of Stalag Luft I hut. Courtesy of Stephan J. M. Scherer.

POWs, in fact, is not possible any longer! Good weather for an escape; will the headcount be correct tomorrow?

Within the next two days 300 American officers will arrive simultaneously! This will be a hard job, especially for the assistant to V. Miller, who has to take charge of the newly arriving prisoners.

Yesterday evening a tunnel was discovered, which was already completed to the fence. The guys had poured the scooped-out sand into the toilets and sinks and then strongly complained that the sewage system did not work properly! Now those gentlemen have to do the cleaning up themselves under the supervision of the German workers.

Today, you can hardly remain in the rooms facing the west. The whole day long I sat in my office wearing the coat to my raingear. My feet feel like icicles, and I will be glad to get in my bed. The curtains are dancing in the room, as if the windows were open!

Colonel Willibald Scherer (right) with Principal from the Ministry of Air Force (Luftwaffen Ministerum) in 1943. Courtesy of Stephan J. M. Scherer.

But now, my dearest, I want to thank you for two dear letters of the 26th and 27th (and the nice Van Gogh postcard) and the letter with the brown wool mending material.

Today, Else showed me a blue uniform shirt that cannot be repaired. I will send it to you, if I get a chance, by post; pieces of it may be useful for making summer shirts for Stephan; recently I had to present a shirt of the same quality in Straubing.

How are things with you? Again you report being worn out, as you have done recently! So the symptoms of your illness have not yet been expelled from your body? Maybe you should try a Brunnenkur* at home? I wonder what doctor can give you the best advice and where you can get x-rayed?

---

*"Brunnenkur" not translatable.

Hopefully you will get over this. Will Agnes be leaving you soon?

Now . . . about [your brother] Stephan: Hopefully you will receive official documents concerning him. Actually, he could be useful to me as a civilian translator. I'm trying hard to locate translators. Presently I have put in a request for 9 people such as him from the translator's school in Bonn-Heigelaar, where their school is located.

That Straubing, and the surrounding area, are fed up with the refugee situation, I can understand; even so it may not be unlikely that people from Vienna will be evacuated that far.

We don't have any fears here and are living as if in the deepest peace. Our foot soldiers have no idea how nice they have it here. What will our comrades in the east have to suffer now!—

Very soon now I shall retreat from this day and therefore close with a heartfelt good night for you and Stephan.

With deep love
Yours, Willi

PS.—Say "Hello" to Agnes as well.

PART VII

Injured and Killed in Action
and Caretakers on the Front Line

S./Sgt. Bill Donofrio was inducted on May 1, 1942, and discharged on February 18, 1946; he served in the U.S. Army for two and a half years before going overseas. After serving in three other divisions, the air corps, and the quartermaster corps, he got overseas by volunteering for the infantry. He was a staff sergeant squad leader in Company E, 274th Infantry Regiment, Seventieth Infantry Division, which entered combat in Alsace, France, on December 28, 1944. Only ten days later, on January 6, 1945, he was wounded in the hand and wrist in the attack on the village of Wingen. Recalling that time, Staff Sergeant Donofrio says the Seventieth were a brand-new division whose training had been cut short and that they met and fought an elite SS unit. Though they won the battle, in three days they suffered 134 casualties out of a battalion of 800. For their action, the battalion was awarded the Presidential Unit Citation. Staff Sergeant Donofrio, who now lives in Florida, wrote letters home relating his injury and subsequent thirteen-month hospitalization.

France
8 January 1945

Dear Mom,

I am asking the Chaplain to write this for me. I guess I forgot to duck and caused a Jerry to hit me, but I was lucky for it was only my hand. I'm in a hospital now, probably will be for quite a while. But there is nothing to worry about and I shall be up and about soon. Do not worry when you get the telegram from the War Dept. I hope this letter gets to you before the wire. Please write to Mary Reilly, 516 Bainbridge St., Brooklyn, NY and tell her about it. Please do not be anxious now, for I am getting the best possible care. Shall write again soon.

All my love,
Will

Jan 17, 1945

Dear Mom,

Here I go trying to write left-handed. As you can see, the results aren't too good. Anyway, the important thing is that I'm OK. So you won't think I'm holding out on you, this is the deal—the bullets that hit me broke bones in my hand and wrist. My hand and wrist are in a cast and probably will be for a while. After that it probably means strengthening the fingers and wrist.

In the meantime, I get the best of care and food. Can you imagine? White blankets and sheets! Some class!

By the way, all the medical staff here came over on the same ship I did. Didn't take long to get together again, did it? I've got no kick coming though. I got off lucky, and I'm not fooling.

That's all for this time, Mom. Take care of yourself and give my love to everyone.

Love,
Will

Jan 22, 1945

Dear Mom,

Here goes another attempt at writing. I'm coming along fine, but as I've told you, it will take time. I'm not going anywhere, so I'm not in any particular rush. You know how lazy I am so you can see how this life agrees with me. I visit some of my buddies here, go to the movies and in general lead a pretty soft existence.

By the way, I was awarded the Purple Heart. A nurse friend of mine was kind enough to mail it home for me. Now show it to those rotten neighbors who were so damned concerned about me not going overseas sooner. Let me know what they say now. Probably, they'll be all sympathy, the damned hypocrites.

Don't worry about me, your lil boy is doing OK. Take care of yourself and give my love to everyone.

Love,
Will

Feb 9, 1945

Dear Mom,

I feel ambitious today, so I'll write my own letter. I usually take advantage of my nurse friend. Which reminds me, have you received my Purple Heart yet? She mailed it for me and as I understand it, she also wrote you a letter. What was in it, I don't know.

I'm not sure, but I think Johnny is here in France. I wrote to him the other day and I hope I see him before I leave here.

I haven't heard from Larry recently, but I hear he's doing OK.

A couple of Majors from our outfit came in to see me the other day. They gave me the order entitling me to wear the Combat Infantryman Badge. That means $10 more every month. Our Battalion received a commendation for its good work when we first met up with the Jerries.

My mail still takes quite some time to catch up with me. By the way, that package you sent me when I was at Fort Wood finally caught up with me. Believe it or not, the cookies were still pretty fresh.

My hand is still in a cast, but it's coming along fine. It doesn't even bother me. As usual, all I do is take things easy.

That's all, Mom, take care of yourself and give my love to everyone.

Love,

Will

• • •

Maj. John Kneisel was born on April 17, 1912, in New York City. He served with the U.S. Army Medical Corps as a combat surgeon with the 105th Portable Surgical Hospital—a Harvard University unit—which was attached to the Thirty-second Division's Regimental Combat Team, and he commanded the unit in 1944 and 1945 as a major. The 105th was organized in Australia and was involved in the battles in New Guinea, the invasion of Morotai in the Moluccas (Dutch East Indies), the landing at Leyte Gulf in the Philippines, and the campaign to liberate the Philippines from the Japanese. At the time of this letter, Major Kneisel had been preparing for the invasion of Japan, but Hiroshima and Nagasaki brought about a quick Japanese surrender and he was allowed to go home. After the war, he was a cardiovascular surgeon, associate clinical professor of surgery at Yale, and chief of surgery at St. Raphael's Hospital in New Haven, Connecticut.

He died on the fourth of July 1997 in Boston. His son, Peter J. Kneisel of Massachusetts, contributed the following letter written by Major Kneisel to his family in California.

[Excerpt]

3 June 1945
Philippines

Dearest Folks—

. . . . I really don't deserve a vacation after this—for we are, as I've told you, running the hospital for a rest camp. There is little work. And the surroundings are as idyllic as many I'd go miles to obtain in the states. We are set up in fine, dry, hard sand in a shady coconut grove. Although the noon heat is worse than [in] New Guinea, the nights are quite cool because of the sea breeze. The bay is framed in lovely mountains. The sea is clear, a fine bathing beach has been bulldozed. There is a swing concert by the fine division orchestra every night—a dance every fourth night. Movies almost every night. Cold Cook (without carbonated water). Frequent steaks and chickens. Ice cream dropped by parachute every fourth night. We are served from plates by Filipino attendants—there are tablecloths (our hospital sheets, of course)—and several Red Cross workers always in attendance. There are native sailing canoes, bankas, available on the beach. Boy, when the army decides the men need a rest, it really provides it for them. On the other hand, I believe that the vastly improved food in part reflects the end of the European war—I think these fellows ought to get better food here from now on—and that's a nice thought.

Why do I describe all this to you? Well as a prelude to a lot of confused thoughts that have been running about in my mind lately. Mostly having to do with my reception at home. I'd like to tell you a number of things I might not find it possible to state when I meet you. One is that the simple fact of coming home and seeing you all again is the be-all and the end-all; I need nothing else. I know that I've had a much easier time than you have. I'm so grateful to the gods for getting me through this without injury or death that the mere fact of returning is more than its own reward. I've really done little—and I want to impress that on you. I've been more fortunate than many in having an opportunity to see a bit more action than the average. But in that action I've done nothing outstanding. Many have. I've given nothing but time. Many, a hell of a lot, have given inestimably more. I feel guilty to think that the experience has been useful to me in my life's work—for that experience has meant more grief for many than I'd like to think about. My only solace is that I have been able to save, I like to think, a fairly decent number of lives in this mess, and maybe lessened the extent of the injuries of another number. But I've lost plenty, too, and I don't feel any too proud about <u>that</u>. The one thing that makes me feel somewhat easier is the fact that while I've engaged in no heroic actions, I've never failed to do my job, and we've never hesitated to set up the hospital in any position where it was needed. But while opportunity plays a large part in magnitude of service, the other fact, that no outstandingly great service has been rendered, must be borne in mind. Thus, I shall have the complete happiness of being able to return with a clear conscience, and a feeling of having never refused an assignment, and of having carried out more of them in fairly credible fashion. But I also bear, as I have just said, the knowledge that my contribution has been minimal compared with many—and consequently—the less said about it, the less embarrassment. . . .

See you soon—all my love.

. . .

Elizabeth Burke was born on November 13, 1919, in Johnson City, New York. During the war, she served in the American Red Cross Overseas Program. She was assigned to Clubmobile duty and served ground troops in England, France, and Germany from June 1944 until October 1945, in the

"Asheville." She and her crew made doughnuts and coffee and took them and American music to soldiers who were just off the front line for a day or two. She followed the army's progress from England, through France and Belgium, and into Germany and often served within a mile or two of the front to give the combat soldiers a short break. Ms. Burke received the Bronze Star Medal. At the time the following letter was written, she was either in Belgium or in Alsace-Lorraine. She was dedicated to serving the foot soldiers who were directly involved in combat. She fancied one soldier in particular, Lt. Francis Niles, who served in the Third Army, Eighty-seventh Infantry Division. His regiment participated in the Battle of the Bulge, crossing the Moselle and then the Rhine at Koblenz on March 25, 1945. He also received a Bronze Star and a Presidential Unit Citation. Elizabeth and Francis married in 1946. The following letter by Ms. Burke was contributed by their daughter, Jean Niles of Texas, and her family. After the war, Ms. Burke worked for a few months at her previous job as a news reporter for the Binghamton Press. *After her marriage, she did not join the workforce again until the mid-seventies, when her husband died. She became a consultant for the Upper Catskill Community Council on the Arts and was elected alderman for her ward in the city of Oneonta, New York. She died in 1982 in Oneonta.*

[Excerpt]

Thursday, Feb. 7

Dear Peg,

. . . . I just returned from church and was much impressed by the attendance. The sermon was not so good but it made an impression and I think most of us think a little more about life and its ultimate end over here. Not that I'm in danger—far from it. But it is the psychology of knowing that just a matter of miles away fellows are killing and being killed because human beings are not human at all. The intelligence we credit ourselves with having doesn't seem to register the fact that man

Elizabeth Burke. Courtesy of Jean A. Niles.

should be able to live peacefully together. But here I go—on a soapbox again.

We have been serving a bunch of fellows fresh from the states and as I once started to tell Barbara—the difference from those who have seen combat is tremendous. Having just finished serving a group of war-weary infantrymen before these new groups I can't help comparing them. The fresh boys are well-mannered and take two doughnuts a customer and are happy to take the cigarettes and candy we offer. They seem to go for the Lifesavers, something combat men seldom do because they've had practically nothing but them overseas. Then, too, the new troops are very polite, orderly and quiet and want to talk to us mainly to find out how far from the front they are, ask if we've been bombed and many other questions like that. They are enthusiastic but a bit scared as one can see.

However, serving a group of men who have been overseas longer is much different. They come up to be served with a whoop and a holler and invariably, though they know they are supposed to limit themselves to two doughnuts, try to fill their pockets and some have a terrific handspan on a doughnut tray. So we have to keep up a regular chant—"Two apiece, please." Another favorite trick is getting on the end of the line and going back. We have to watch that, too, because in serving thousands of men it takes much time to make enough doughnuts.

Then, too, you'll be surprised at the effect of combat on our manhood. Everyone ages about four years and many age much more. A fellow walked into the Clubmobile one night when we were out serving and we got talking about age. Of course, they try to kid me about being 19, etc., but I'm not fooled by it. (The crow's feet around my eyes aren't fading and I now have two definite wrinkles in my neck.) Anyway, this fellow asked me to guess his age. I knew he must be young because most infantrymen are but I finally settled for twenty-two, though he really looked about thirty. He told me he was twenty and it really was a shock to me. Of course we usually see them under adverse conditions—they are dirty and haven't shaven for days. They usually have been traveling in boxcars and their array of clothing is really something to see. Anything goes to keep warm and that is literal. It usually is hard to identify officers from enlisted men, too. They are all just weary Americans.

It's a different world over here. Sometimes I can't believe that so much is going on while we go placidly on making coffee and doughnuts and feeding groups of men whom we probably never will see again. After a while, one gets so that all faces seem more or less alike and pass on and on in endless rows. The individuality of a man or woman is taken away by a uniform and I often wonder just what kind of person I happen to be serving a cup of coffee or giving gum and cigarettes and candy. . . .

Loads of love,
Burke

• • •

Lt. Lucille Backemeyer and Marv and Doris Weber attended the same church, and all went to school together in Nebraska. Doris (Weber) McCallister of Nebraska, who contributed Lieutenant Backemeyer's letter, tells me she received it when her husband, Lt. Marvin C. Weber, was stationed at Camp Campbell in Kentucky shortly before he was shipped overseas. (Please see Part I: The Battles for a letter by Lieutenant Weber.) Lieutenant Backemeyer was one of two dieticians with the Thirty-sixth General Hospital in the Army Medical Corps attached to the Fifth Army. At the time she was on temporary duty in Naples. Lieutenant Backemeyer now lives in California.

Lieutenant Lucille Backemeyer (left) with Lieutenant Ruby Lysen in Caserta, Italy, in October 1943. Courtesy of Doris S. McCallister.

July 20th, 1944

Dear Marv and Dory:

You write the "newsiest" letters I get—wish there were more of them. My own answers to my mail always sound so dull to me I marvel that any of my friends bother to answer.

Your husband's in a fine division now. Tell him to be proud of it— and if the 20th goes through as much, and as well, as some of the earlier divisions of the same type that I have known here in Italy, they have a high record to shoot at.

Speaking of hovels and homes, since I have been in the army I have lived in regulation army barracks (one- and two-storey types); in pyramidal tents (with and without floors)—in and out of mud; in a former insane hospital (part of the patients still there); a French villa with a personal maid; Italian prisoner barracks (with rats); prefabricated houses; a sulfur bath resort; and a bombed-out building with no roof—no beds—no blankets—just the floor and stars (take it back, no stars; that was in the rainy season). My recent acquisition is a transient hotel that I'm helping run. We have either private rooms (only ten to a room) or double rooms (with 18 people sharing the floor space). The outstanding feature about our hotel is that we have bigger and more fleas than anyplace in the city, and that our location is in the center of the most flourishing red-light district!

I have easy access to a large outdoor market, so typical of Italy. I buy a lot of fresh fruits and vegetables for the hotel mess, and seem, as a general rule, to keep the little chicks fairly happy.

It's 11 o'clock and my bedtime is past due. Long, hard day tomorrow. So good nite.

Love,
Lucy

• • •

Sgt. Paul R. Lewis served with the U.S. Army, Eighty-third Infantry Division, 330th Infantry, Third Batallion, Company K, as mortarman in a rifle company. He was in the infantry for the second wave on Omaha Beach with Gen. Omar Bradley's First Army until Gen. George Patton brought his tanks in and Sergeant Lewis joined the Third Army, went to Paris, and transferred to the Ninth Army. He was captured by German forces in Huertgen Forest on December 11, 1944. He remained a prisoner of war in Stalag 12A until April 13, 1945, when he was liberated. His daughter, Georgeanna Slaybaugh of Indiana, who contributed this letter that Private First Class Lewis wrote to his wife, says, "When he recovered from his ordeal, in an ironic twist of fate, Dad was sent back to Camp Atterbury as a sergeant over the German prisoners of war being held at the facility."

Luxembourg
Nov 11, 1944

Dear Corky,

As I sit here writing this my mind wanders back two years ago this very day. It was Wednesday and at 9:30 in the morning I became a soldier. For a year and a half I trained for the job I was chosen to fulfill in this war.

I have been all over since then, seen plenty too. Some things will remain on my mind until the day I die. A lot of the boys I used to sleep and eat with are no more. To a lot of people they are just a lot of wooden crosses in an open field. But to me they were the best pals a guy ever had. I wish as I write this that I could tell you just what the score is. But my lips are sealed—only God knows my inner thoughts. These things keep turning over and over in my mind. When will this war end? How long will it be before we can come back home? Will I ever be the same? Will you be willing to forget what I am when I come back home? I am a killer, honey! I have killed men who didn't even know right from wrong. I wonder if in the eyes of God we are in the right. I am not perfect nor do I claim to be, but in my own way I think I am right. I have done nothing yet that I am ashamed of. I remember how you cried when I came back that morning and told you I was in the Army. I wasn't in the Army long before Connie was born. She sure was cute! It has been a long time since I've seen her. I wonder if she will know me when I come back? I love you both so much, honey. It hurts and hurts plenty to be away from home and loved ones.

They call us brave men, honey, the backbone of the Army. But it is for our loved ones back home we are fighting so hard. Yes we want peace as soon as can be so we can return home to start life anew. We can't start from where we left off because times have changed. We have changed too, honey. Growing older and wiser everyday. I have plans, honey— great ones if only God will permit my safe return home. It's going to be a tough winter, honey. I hope the war is over before winter ends. Chin up, honey. I hope to be with you again someday.

Your loving husband,
Pfc. Paul R. Lewis

• • •

Cpl. Aubert F. Seguin served with the U.S. Army, 410th Infantry Regiment, 103rd Infantry Division, in the European theater of operations. This letter home to his wife's parents was written upon learning of the death of his brother-in-law, Pvt. Donald H. Emrick, a combat medic with the 335th Infantry Regiment, 84th Infantry Division, who was killed during the Battle of the Bulge on January 22, 1945. Corporal Seguin's son, Kenneth E. Seguin, a lieutenant colonel in the United States Air Force Reserve of Texas, shared this letter.

Corporal Aubert F. Seguin. Courtesy of Kenneth E. Seguin.

Sunday, February 25, 1945

Dearest Mom & Dad—

Rec. Shirley's letter telling me of Donald's death. Was so very sorry to hear of it. It must be awfully hard on a mother & father to lose a child. If you could only say, "Well, I've still got 10 left." But that don't work, because each & every one is as near & dear to your hearts as the next one. I know how close Dad & Donald were, too. But can you think of any better way of giving his life than for his country? Mom, you've got to remember that someone's got to die in this war. This game is for keeps. If it hadn't been Don, it would have been some other young man, & his mother would be just as sorrowful. It's a chance each one of us is taking, gambling our lives for the Germans' lives. But then, we don't kill medics, so it shows we're not as barbarian as they are. God must have wanted him now, or he would have let Donald live.

You know, Mom, maybe Don could have found some kind of job back home that would have kept him there. But he wouldn't have felt right about it. And besides, that adventuresome spirit never left him. And because you raised him from a kid, & knew everything about him, you're sure & certain that he was an allright guy. You can bet that whatever he was doing, it was a good job.

Don't feel too badly; it'll take a while to forget it, maybe a long while. But remember, he gave his all, & he couldn't do more. Try to think of other things & when you begin to think of him, don't cry, but remind yourself that his time came & there was nothing you could do to stop it.

All my love to you. I remember you in all my prayers. Write when you can.

Love,
Aubert

PART VIII

The End of the War

Keith B. Lynch (rank unknown) wrote this letter home to Nebraska from the U.S.S. Ruticulus *and sent it from Nagasaki, Kyushu, Japan. He died in 1996. His wife, Lorraine Lynch of Nebraska, contributed the letter.*

U.S.S. Ruticulus AK-113
Nagasaki, Kyushu, Japan

Sunday, September 23, 1945

Dear Folks:

Here it is Sunday, Holiday Routine again. Boy, does the time fly. It seems as if it were only yesterday that I sat out here topside of the veranda and wrote the last time. We've gotten mail twice this week and I've my share, eight of them. The last one I got was mailed the 10th of September, the same day we left Okinawa. A letter in twelve days. That's not so bad.

Well, to come to one of the two main topics I am to discuss (like they say in the movies): yesterday I went on my first, and most likely only, liberty in Nagasaki. The crew was divided into six sections and one went every hour. Each tour lasted two hours. We went to the beach and were put in trucks and given a tour of the city of Nagasaki. First we visited the main part of the city. It wasn't [the main part], but is now, as it wasn't hurt so much by the atomic bomb. The only activity you see is people walking, going nowhere, it seems. Just walking.

Now I know what they mean when they say, "Dead City." You remember when I first described the place to you? About the city being in two valleys going at right angles to each other from the harbor, with a string of mountains between them? The smaller of the two, about the same size and five or six times the population of Tecumseh, was the first we visited. It was damaged of course by the concussion of the atomic blast and also by two previous bombings. But the main part of the place, in the other valley, about the size of Lincoln I would say, and five or six times the population, was completely inundated. The sight I saw from the top of the hill, over which it was approximated the center of the blast, was a sight I hope my children, if I am so fortunate, will never have to see, hear of, or ever think of. It was horrible and when you get to thinking, unbelievable. To think that a thirty-pound bomb the size of a basketball, exploding a thousand feet in the air, could cause such a holocaust was simply unbelievable. I shudder to think what these people underwent when the blast occurred. A blast that literally dissolved their homes, family, friends and any other material thing in the vicinity. A blast that pushed over huge steel structures a mile and a half away as if they were made of blocks. Now I can see what they mean when they say, "Dead City." A city with no buildings, no trees, no facilities, and no people. All you see from the top of the hill is ground covered with bricks, burned wood, twisted and pushed over steel frames of buildings for several miles in each direction. There is nothing for the people of this "Dead City" to do but walk around and think, "What manner of people would do such a thing to us, who are a peaceful, courteous, and civilized people?" I wondered what they thought when they looked at us as we were driving along. "Are these the barbarians who did such a thing to us? What can we expect now that we are at their mercy?" I only wish they could be made to suffer a tenth of the atrocities that they performed on our men whom they held prisoner. People can say these people are simple, ignorant of the facts, or under a spell, but a nation cannot wage war as they have without the backing of the majority of their people.

Such a thing as I saw yesterday cannot be described in words. You have to see it and I hope no one ever has to see such a thing again.

Well, I found out that my enlistment expires next March. If I get out then it'll just about be right. Here's hoping. Well, folks, I've got a couple other letters to write before the movie. I'll see if I can't get another letter off before next Sunday.

'Til then,

Love,

Son

• • •

SN1 Jack Burgeman volunteered for the U.S. Navy in February 1943 and was discharged in January 1945. He served aboard the battleship U.S.S. Alabama for twenty-nine months at sea, beginning in August 1943. Seaman First Class Burgeman was a range finder operator in one of three mounts of sixteen-inch, sixty-foot guns. Each shell weighed between two thousand and three thousand pounds and had a distance of twenty miles. He also served on one of the forty-millimeter antiaircraft guns. The U.S.S. Alabama shot down approximately twenty-five kamikazes and spent the last sixty-seven days of the war bombarding the Japanese homeland, firing upon kamikaze attacks, and also firing at two-men suicide submarines. They also fired at baka bombs made up of humans attached to bombs. Once they saw an armada of U.S. B-29s flying toward Japanese cities, dipping their wings to the members of the fleet; one of the planes was the Enola Gay. The following letter was written four days after the Japanese surrendered. It was stamped with a cover honoring all the men who were there at that time in commemoration of V-J Day. It was written to his brother, who was serving in the U.S. Army Air Force at Lowry Field in Denver, Colorado. Sergeant First Class Burgeman now lives in Illinois.

Seaman First Class Jack Burgeman aboard ship in 1944. Courtesy of Jack Burgeman.

Sept. 6, 1945
Tokyo Bay

Dear Clarence,

They've finally knocked off censorship.

Well, Clare, our stay of 67 straight days continually at sea was culminated by us by dropping the hook (anchoring) in Tokyo Bay. It sure makes our blood curdle with delight. It's been a long winding road from the Gilberts to Tokyo, but we made it with victory for us and an ignominious defeat for the Japs. Our ship led the procession of battleships & cruisers in. You see as I told you before that now with Rear Admiral Shafroth aboard we are flagship of all the new battleships in the fleet. Coming into the Bay, some Jap sandpans came close enough to gaze upon our triumphant procession—every one of their crew was straining their eyes by focusing their glasses on us with daze & awe. Some of their ships are sunk & half sunk in this harbor, including the famous battleship Nogoto.

Today our landing force of 200 sailors came back; they were on the homeland for five days guarding the Naval base, caves, and ammunition dumps, communication centers, etc. They all had many a good yarn to spill & beautiful souvenirs. Before congregating again with us they were all deloused. You see, every big ship of the fleet had to supply men to make up a landing force of Navy personnel to land in conjunction with MacArthur's men.

The famous admiral, Richard E. Byrd, was aboard our ship for about two weeks some time back. He was an observer for the night bombardment of the city of Hitashi that took place a while back. I have his photograph too in my war diary. He is a real man; a man's man. This letter is enclosed in an envelope which is a first day cover or cachet commemorating VJ day. Save it, Clare!! It's a good souvenir & someday it may have a certain value. I hope that I can be home for your wedding. We expect to be home for Navy Day.

Your loving bro,

Jerry

. . .

Cpl. Cyril J. Charters was a projectionist with the Thirty-seventh Royal Army Ordnance Corps Kinema Section, between July 1944 and August 1945. He wrote home of the Normandy landings and of the advance through northern France, Belgium, and northern Germany. The following letter was written from Belsen in 1945, a month or so after the liberation of the former concentration camp while he was serving with the British Liberation Army. The letter was contributed by his wife, Eileen Charters, of Plymouth, England.

13057038 Cpl Charters C.J.
37, Kinema Section RAOC
B.L.A.
Letter No. 39
Tuesday 15th May 1945

Written in Belsen Concentration Camp:

My darling,

The other day you told me you were going to the film of Belsen "Horror" camp. Many people throughout England will see the film. Few will have missed seeing the pictures in the papers. Yet, how many, I wonder, will really believe it true? How many will say "Propaganda"? How many will think that the poor creatures shown in these pictures have been specially selected? All too many I'm afraid. Yet here, as I write this letter within the camp, is the dreadful evidence to show that the accounts are only lacking truth by concealment of terrible facts and sights which decency itself forbids publishing.

With ironic humour I realise that I should possibly have been the first to cry out: "Propaganda!—selected pictures!" if I had seen the pictures in England, but, like St. Thomas, the proof has been put before my eyes. Those pictures that have shocked the world are nothing in comparison to that ghost-like army that line the corridors and fill the rooms of Belsen. They lie in their beds mute and helpless, with fleshless limbs grotesquely protruding from under the blankets. Lifeless eyes glare out of hollow spaces devoid of flesh; their necks are thinner than my wrist. But I cannot describe the fearful sight. Try to picture a skeleton covered with skin alone; try to picture a skeleton like that with the faintest spark of life in it; try to picture thousands like it ravaged with typhus, dysentery and even worse diseases—picture that in your mind and you know, in part, the truth of Belsen.

Yesterday, walking along a corridor, I heard a hoarse, half-whispered voice murmur "Comrade!," as though the whisperer was trying to assure himself that he really was in safe hands. I turned and smiled at him with sympathy and friendliness; but his next word struck a chord within me that made me feel sick with helplessness and compassion. It was the simple word—"Bread," uttered with all the fervour and pleading of a starving man.

Bread, the staff of life, that would bring death to him as surely as a knife thrust if given to him in that condition.

"Soon!" I answered softly, and walked away.

Later in the evening a medical sister was crying. She had tended some of the most fearful wounds, and had seen death in its most hideous forms and had not flinched; but now she was crying—another one had died. "Yes, Sister," her ward-orderly soothed, "but they are all dying. We must expect this."

The medical world has thrown everything into an all-out battle to bring back these living skeletons to life and health again. Hospitals and medical units work unceasingly. Every available unit has been rushed in until the whole district looks like one huge hospital. 100 students from London hospitals are here. The less than 400 German nurses and 40 doctors are helping in this tremendous struggle.

Yet, as I write this, I can see two great clusters of communal graves. One, in the far corner of the field, is marked by nine black crosses. It was done during the German reign of terror and I dread to think of the thousands who are buried there. The other is but twenty-five yards in front of me where white crosses stand over long, flat-shaped mounds. These latter graves contain the victims who were dead, or have died, since the liberation of the camp. Two thousand bodies lie there.

Across the field I know there is a cemetery already more than half-filled; each day sees more graves added.

And there are others, not forgetting the horrible incinerator.

The full story of Belsen has yet to be written, but when the day dawns of its publication this most brutal, inhuman and ghastly Hell on earth will be revealed to the whole world. I have mentioned nothing of what happened in Belsen before its liberation by the Allies, nor of the sights that met our soldiers' gaze when first they entered, for here I tell you only of my own personal experience of the place.

I do not believe in gloating and publishing the sins of another whether that other be a man or a nation, but this is a crime of which the whole world should know; a crime more fiendish, more cold-blooded and calculated than the "Black Hole of Calcutta."

I wish I could put this letter in the "Western Independent" that Westcounty folk could have a Westcounty man's testimony for the truth of what they have read and seen in papers and on films.

I wish all men connected with this camp would write home to their folks and local papers and substantiate the truth.

But, above all, I wish that every possible German could be conducted around the camp to see with his own eyes what his blind faith and idolatry of the Nazi creed made possible, or what his fear allowed to continue.

Now, rising above the green of tree and woodland, a column of black rolling smoke ascends, to gradually disperse and blend with the clouds, the first block of Belsen's huts has been fired—Germany is being cleansed of one of its blackest spots; but the crime has yet to be cleansed.

Cheerio, my darling,
Your own
Cyril XXX
(13057038 Cpl Charters C.J.)

. . .

Pvt. Dural McCombs wrote this letter to his cousin after his company, the 162nd Infantry, Company B, went to Japan after the bombing of Hiroshima and Nagasaki; they were the first American company to enter the country. Private McCombs's cousin, Evelyn McCombs Deike of California, shared this letter.

Pvt. Dural McCombs
39429280 Co. B
162nd. Inf. A.P.O. 41
c/o P.M. San Francisco, Calif.

Miss Evelyn McCombs
2010 Parker St.
Berkeley, Calif.
Humbolt County

Kiue, Japan
Oct. 29—45

Dear Evelyn,

Please excuse the mistakes as this is all the paper I have.

I rec. your letter yesterday and was glad to hear from you. Our mail is just now catching up with us and we got here the 6th.

We got off the boat about 6 o'clock and marched out here to where we are staying now—about 2 miles. We were the first bunch to come in here except a couple of officers who had come in on a plane.

When we got off the boat we formed up in our Platoons and started down the road. When we came through town they had everybody off the streets and [it] was guarded so that we would have full right of way. The town was really quiet—no one talking—the Police just standing there not even batting an eye. All you could hear was us just marching

Private Dural McCombs (bottom row, third from left) in Zamboanga, Philippines, 1945. Courtesy of Evelyn McCombs Deike.

down the street. It was quieter than a funeral. I don't know what made it seem so weird but I never said much about it till the next day and everybody felt the same thing.

Now though the Nips don't seem to be afraid of us. Now when you go to town the kids pretty near knock you down trying to get candy, gum and cigarettes.

The people bow and salute you. I don't know why they do that when I know they don't like us. They seem to have lots of money but nothing to buy. They sure do try to get stuff from the G.I.'s and I guess they must be doing it, too, as now some fellows seem to have too much money and we haven't been paid for over 2 months. Now you can't send but so much money home and you won't be able to take but so much back. What they are trying to do is stop the black market. Cigarettes were selling for a hundred yen a carton and it takes 15 yen to make 1 U.S. dollar so they were getting pretty near $7.00 a carton and they were issued to us.

They have some nice kimonos here. Some of the boys have gotten some but they are pretty high. The men don't seem to have too many clothes but the women (most of them) seem to have pretty nice clothes. They wear kind of bloomer pants or something. They are big and baggy until about the knees and then they are right tight down to the ankles. They sure do look funny and they wear wooden slippers—usually they don't have any socks. They really work too, haul wagons and carts and some of them pack packs that look like they would break their backs but I guess it doesn't.

I have been on guard since yesterday at 3 o'clock and I just got off. We are on about 2½ hours and are off about 3½ but after we eat we don't have much chance to sleep so I am a little sleepy. I was guarding an old tunnel that was full of powder. It was not far from Hiroshima. I was up to Hiroshima the other day to see where the atomic bomb was dropped. I can't explain just what it was like, but the whole city is just gone; there is just a pile of rubbish there now. All the iron and steel things were destroyed; it seems to work more on metal than anything [else]. We stopped and got out in one place and looked around. There didn't seem to be much of anything there, just rubbish and bones of dead Nips.

You could stand there in the middle of where the city used to be and look in any direction and all you could see is rubbish. It really is worth seeing. Something that I probably won't ever forget. I sure would like to have some pictures of it.

For miles outside the city the windows were all broken out of the houses. I'll bet that was a pretty place at one time as there are some pretty places on the road up there.

Well today for the first time since we have been here we got a good meal. We have been eating rations but now we are getting some good grub and mail and now we are to move again [on] the first and where we are going it is supposed to be away back from good roads, etc. so probably our mail and grub situation will be pretty poor again for awhile.

Well, guess I'd better close for now and go to bed. Please write once in awhile as I sure like to get letters. Just ask me questions if you want to and maybe I can cover answers then as I probably will have a hard time trying to write.

Oh, yes, that girl used to go to school with you—she was a year or so behind you—her name if I can spell it right was KAPYR. I used to see her up at Dow's Prairie.

Well, I guess I will not go to sleep till after supper as we have to stand retreat tonight. We always do on week nights but usually you don't if you are on guard.

Well, so long for now and good luck.

As ever,

Dural

• • •

Capt. Mazzini Grimshaw volunteered for army service in 1941. He enlisted in the British Royal Artillery but was commissioned into the Royal Army Service Corps in May 1942 as a junior officer. In November 1942 he was a part of Operation Torch, the North Africa landings, and landed at Algiers. In October 1943 he was in a follow-up unit of Operation Slapstick, landing at Taranto in southern Italy. He remained in the Salerno, Italy, area until December 1945, when he was sent home on compassionate leave because of the death of his father. The following letter by Captain Grimshaw, which was submitted by his daughter, Anne Grimshaw of Hatfield, England, was written from Italy soon after the end of war to his sister in England.

Captain Grimshaw's daughter says that she went in 1988 to the Commonwealth War Graves Commission military cemetery in Salerno, Italy, following her father's instructions in the letter, that she found the grave of John Fairbrother, and that she, too, put flowers on it, "just as Dad said he would do forty-three years before."

Captain Mazzini Grimshaw after commission as second lieutenant in Royal Army Service Corps, May 1942. Courtesy of Anne Grimshaw.

Capt. M. Grimshaw R.A.S.C.
766 Coy. R.A.S.C. (GT)
C.M.F.

5th Oct. 45.

Dear Annie and Joe:

Thank you very much for the parcel of cigs just received, Senior Service, just the job. Please don't send any more now the price has risen; they are not worth it and I can get along with my pipe.

How is Edith [Anne Grimshaw's mother] looking these days? Please let me know what you think about her, if she is looking better.

To-day has been a day of memories. I visited the beaches of Picciola, the villages of Battipaglia and Pontecagnano and on to the military cemetery, which is at Pontecagnano. It was 1430 hrs when I arrived at the factory at Picciola and leaving the car I walked down to the beach. The sun was shining and it was very warm. The sky was blue and the sea calm. I walked in the direction of Salerno for about a mile along the road I knew so well and as I looked ahead I could see the Sorrento peninsula cutting the sky with its rugged but beautiful outline. I looked out to sea and saw a few yachts with their white sails in the breeze and the fishermen pulling in their nets. There were a few children about. It was peaceful.

What a contrast to the scene of the morning of the 9th Sept 43. The sea crowded with ships of all types. The LST's with their bows open on the beach like huge whales disgorging instruments of death, thunderous noises from the Naval guns, beach officers shouting their orders through megaphones, men running forward some never to return. Hell, it seems like a nightmare.

As I walked back along the road I was overcome with a sense of gratitude.

I arrived at the cemetery about 1700. It is very neat and tidy with a low stone wall, a simple kind of gate at the entrance and as you enter there is a wide drive up the centre at the top of which stands a flagstaff with the Union Jack hoisted. On each side of this path are rows and rows of graves, hundreds, so neat and well kept, each with a white marble cross bearing the name and regiment of the soldier buried there. It did not take me long to find the grave. Fairbrother's, and if they would like particulars you might pass this on to them. It is Plot 2, Row C, Grave 47. If you will let me have the particulars of the other young man's I will make another visit and take a few flowers along. After [ward] I saw the Officer in charge and asked him if it was permissable to place a small tablet of some description on graves. He said there was no order against it but they tried to keep them all the same, which I think is the right thing and I think you would agree if you could see them. There is no distinction between Officers and men, rich or poor— just as it should be.

Well, what do you think of the latest demob' news? Looks as if I have "had it"! If you are thinking of buying a turkey for my Xmas party I suggest you get one in a tin and then I can have it at Easter. I feel very angry about it; well, that's putting it mild. I am wondering what is to happen to all those who have never been out of England.

That, I fear, is all for now. Please write and let me have that information as quickly as possible.

Cheerio and good luck.

Yours sincerely,

Mazzini

P.S. When I look at this effort it makes me feel clever . . . ?
M.

. . .

Dr. Eugene E. Eckstam entered the U.S. Navy on January, 10, 1944, immediately following his internship. On April 28, 1944, he was involved with the "practice exercise" called Exercise Tiger, during which his ship and another were struck, with a loss of 639 men—the largest number of casualties during a single naval engagement during World War II. After being reassigned to another ship, Dr. Eckstam and his unit invaded Omaha Beach the day after D day, but they were forced to wait five days for the army headquarters until going ashore. He was then sent to the Pacific Islands as a lieutenant, Medical Corps, United States Naval Reserve, assigned to Naval Advanced Base Unit Number 11, an advanced base unit, operating with one doctor and three hospital corpsmen to run a sick bay. After the writing of the following letter, Dr. Eckstam was transferred to Manila to a similar unit as a senior medical officer and the liaison for Navy men confined to Army hospitals. After nearly two and a half years on active duty, Dr. Eckstam was discharged in May 1946. Dr. Eckstam now lives in Minnesota.

*Dr. Eugene E. Eckstam upon entering the U.S. Navy
in January 1944. Courtesy of Eugene E. Eckstam.*

Sept. 5, 1945
Iloio, Panay

Hi People.

Now that censorship has been officially released here, it will be hard
to write about everything. I am so used to avoiding certain topics that I
will have trouble including them. If you have any questions to ask list
them all in a letter and I'll answer them. I will help by making a brief
resume of the places I have been.

I sailed from S.F. in the evening of March 1 and saw the Golden
Gate in all its glory. We sailed on the S.S. Mormachawk—a liberty ship
converted into a troop ship. The berths were in the holds of the ship but
there were blowers and it was not too uncomfortable. We carried around
1,500 men and officers over 55 officers were quartered in one room the

size of Aunt Ag's living room. The bunks were 3 high and end to end with narrow aisles. Enlisted men's quarters were 4 high etc.

The islands we stopped at on the way over are as follows: Pearl Harbor for three days and three nice liberties; Eniwetok over-night; boy is that ever a warm place—just a little sand shoal sticking out of the water and only a few trees; we sailed past the Kwajelain group; we saw part of the fleet at Ulithe as we steamed by; we stopped at the north end of the Palau group inside a coral reef for a week. At Palau Japs were still on the island all except for a Marine airstrip, U.S., at the southern end. The Japs on shore could look out at night and see our movies thru binoculars. All the sting had been taken out of them by destroying their large guns, so they were harmless as far as we were concerned. We could see the Marines bombing and strafing the island daily while we were sitting in the harbor reading books and playing cards. Isn't that a silly situation? Still it was a good example of how the U.S. island hopped in the Pacific to get ahead so fast.

We landed on Guinan, Samar about April 8 after about 39 days at sea and the only time we got ashore was at Pearl Harbor. On the 9th my group got immediate orders to report to NABU #11, so we left in an hour. My sea chests went under piles of 2nd and 4th class mail we had brought out, so I couldn't get to them. I spent 4 busy days lining up some medical gear because the transport that carried it was not to due to unload till after we left. I got plenty of supplies to carry us over. While there I also drove down to Calicoan Island and saw Panter, Hofsteen, and Bakkila.

We boarded an LST [Landing Ship Tank] and sailed the 12th for Mindanao. We got there the a.m. of the 17th and saw Naval gunfire and the rockets and then the troops go ashore. By noon we were able to get quite close to shore because the Japs didn't have much fight. In fact there were only a couple hundred there and we never heard from them again.

If you look at a map of Mindanao—Malabang is 35 miles north of

Panay. There the natives were on the beach waving American flags and selling bananas to the troops as they went ashore. As a matter of fact I bought some when I went ashore at Panay—2 days after the initial landing.

The main Jap force had pulled out a couple of days before. We were supposed to invade 10 days later, but when we found how few Japs were left we went in earlier. That 10 days would have given me time to get all my personal and medical gear—so you can see how closely an invasion is timed, and how far in advance. It is really remarkable.

We went ashore the 19th and set up temporary camp and sick bay. Sick bay was in one tent in the mud. It was a week before we got a hot meal and that was luxury at that point after eating K rations. We were darn lucky we had no opposition because we could have eaten K rations for a long time. It was about 5 weeks before we got fresh meat and potatoes. I had almost forgotten what it tasted like. If I ever see any dehydrated foods and carrots, peas, potatoes, or spam I shall SCREAM. I have had so much canned meat [such] as bully beef, lousy-tasting sausages, etc. that I can't look at canned meat anymore. Of course you have to eat something. In general though we have been very fortunate with good eats; I have lost some weight, and was down to about 150 at one time but now I must be about 160–165 with no pot tummy. Nobody is fat out here, and everyone seems to go thru the same stages.

We left Panay on the 5th of July and got here via LSN on the 8th. This place I have already described as a mud hole without hot [water], and when a bulldozer gets stuck, that's something.

Now take a look at the map of Panay. See Iloio? And the Iloilo River? The former city airport (now used for storage and useless for planes) is on the southern tip of land at the south of the river. We have to drive 2 miles up this side of the river to get to the highway that crosses the river and go into town.

So, now I have brought up most of the things to date and will now tell of the extremely interesting experience I have had in the past few days. I would not be able to tell them except that censorship has been lifted.

All the time we've been here we've known that there were about 400–600 Japs on the island up in the hills. The nearest were about 30 miles away. Once, about a month ago, they made a raid on a native village for supplies. We did not shell them because we would have killed lots of civilians. They retreated again, and we helped the civilians out on their stuff.

After the Japs decided to surrender, negotiations were carried on [on] every island in the Pacific for local surrenders. There are still Japs on nearly every island in the area as here.

Sept. 2 was the day for the formal surrender here and I didn't see that. They were due to come in straggled groups for 2 more days so since I hadn't seen a Jap yet I decided to see one. Harry and I found out that the prison camp was about 13 miles from here so we drove up. I talked with an Army doc and also a Jap doc briefly, and found that the Japs did not have any medical supplies for over a YEAR. I'll go into this later. We didn't have much time so we left soon. The prisoners appeared to be in pretty good shape, but their clothes were a sight—patched and ragged. They looked well-fed though.

While at the camp the Army doc said more were surrendering the next day so guess what we did? Previously the farthest we could go was about a mile beyond the prison camp because they didn't want us to get tangled up with the Japs in any way. Reeder, Kreiser (all in my tent) and I drove up the next day—32 miles away. All along the road we saw guards and got somewhat worried. In fact we had to do some fancy talking at one place to keep from being sent back cause we didn't have a pass to go that far. We found out later that you were supposed to attend by invitation only—from the Army—but we just barged in.

The place we drove to was Lambuao—in the central part of the island. Most of the road was concrete and we buzzed along at 40 miles an hour. Over the gravel and dirt winding roads we had to go slower.

We had to salute all the guards and we were really tired in our right arms when we got back. It took about 1½ hours to get there and we arrived at 9:15 a.m. at the clearing outside the village. All the way up we were wondering if we were on the right road when we didn't see guards every 20 yards, and were wondering what would happen if we should run into a Jap patrol. Gosh, that trip was certainly tense. We found out later that the guards were there to keep the natives from throwing stones at the Japs as they came down in the trucks.

The first group of Japs was just going thru the lines giving up their arms when we arrived. We had plenty of machine guns around, and that didn't look too good either at first. Groups came up in succession out of the jungle on a narrow path. There were about 30–50 in each group led by an officer. They halted just before reaching the clearing and were given instructions by one of the Army officers who spoke Japanese. They had marched up in double columns with full field pack, rifles on their shoulders, belts with canteens, grenades, bullets, bayonets, and knives. Some carried portable machine guns, mortars, etc. All guns had the bolt open and were not loaded; all guns were in good shape.

The Jap officer, after receiving instructions, marched up to the commanding officer's table and presented his Samurai sword and pistols; each officer carried 1–3 pistols. Then they were searched in detail for small knives, etc. Meanwhile the men marched in 2 columns and separated single file past a group of soldiers. Here they gave up in succession their rifle, bayonet, grenades, entrenching tools (small picks and shovels, and other knives and war equipment). Then each was individually searched for small concealed knives and grenades, etc.

Each man carried a sheath knife for hand to hand combat and several small knives. Each man also carried about 6 grenades tied to his belt. Boy, what a lot of trouble could have ensued if a couple grenades had been thrown around. In fact one threw a grenade into a pile of other grenades and equipment, and we almost went nuts for a second. Apparently he decided to throw his own in the pile and save a soldier some trouble cause we were throwing them down too. Fortunately he didn't pull the pin. Grenades will not go off unless the pin is pulled; that sets off the timer, so it is safe to throw them down. I lost about ten years' growth there.

As groups of 200 were collected they were loaded into trucks and taken in convoy to the prison camp some 18 miles down the line. About 470 came in that morning and of these about 50 were ill and a few were stretcher cases. They came in rolled in mats and tied to a pole that two Japs carried. All had come by foot a good distance and many were very weak and some had dropped by the wayside and had to be picked up. They said that about 800 had died in the last 2 months from disease.

Remember the total expected was 400–600 and the final tally was about 1,700. I had my camera along and had 2 rolls of film from a package that arrived the day before (Ruthie and Georgie's, plus the peanuts). My camera jammed—of all days—and I got only 10 out of 16 pictures, but those will be O.K. I have seen the negatives already. I'll send the negatives home soon in a letter with instructions.

The Japs that were well were in very good shape, but those that were sick were very ill. Mostly due to chronic malaria, dysentery, and beri-beri.

While we drove up alone and uninvited and talked our way thru 2 guard posts we came back in a convoy of 17 jeeps and had lunch halfway back.

At the scene there was no joy on our part nor sadness on the Japs'. We were businesslike and the Japs appeared to be confused as if they couldn't comprehend what was going on. There was no arrogance or sneering or any attempt at a revenge stroke; they were very meek but still military in their bearing. They presented as strict a military discipline and appearance as could be expected in their tattered condition.

It was an event in my life that I will never forget. I am certainly glad we had enough guts to go up there and see the Jap surrender on Panay.

I had better stop now and get this in the mail. The day after this I made rounds in the Army hospital here on the Japs' ward and talked with a Jap doctor and I will write back all about this in the next letter.

Incidentally I picked up from some Japs some Jap morphine, a cigarette, and a Bayer aspirin tablet also scribbled on in Jap.

Bye for now.

Love,

Gene

P.S. Remember to list your questions.

• • •

MoMM John M. Ferrary was born on December 20, 1909, in Mount Carmel, Pennsylvania. His family moved to West Paterson, New Jersey, when he was an infant. Annita Zalenski, of New Jersey, who contributed the following letter, received it in 1945 from her uncle when she was nine-years-old. He was stationed in the South Pacific with the U.S. Navy working as a motor machinist mate, third class, on a motor torpedo boat (PT boat). He saw most of his action in the Philippines, where he sent the letter; it was written shortly after V-J Day. At that time, he was working at building a new base camp. He was awarded the Philippine Liberation Ribbon with one star, the Asiatic-Pacific Ribbon, and the World War II Victory Medal. He was discharged in 1945 and returned to his hometown, where he lived with his wife, Agnes. They did not have children. He was a foreman in a stone quarry for many years. He also served on the school board and was active in local politics and in his parish church. With the exception of the time he spent in the service, he lived in the house his father built in 1923 until his death on December 8, 1994.

19 August 1945

Dear Annita,

I am addressing this letter to you but really I am writing to you, Mother and Daddy, so this letter is for all of you. I received two of your letters and one of Mother's this past week and I didn't answer sooner

*Motor Machinist's Mate, Third Class John M.
Ferrary. Courtesy of Annita Zalenski.*

because I've been running around the countryside too much and I am lazy and tired, but here goes now.

This last letter of yours was very nice; you sure are getting to be a very smart girl. I can't wait until I hear you play the piano; also I hope your puppy takes a prize in the pet show. What's the matter with Daddy that he can't paint without leaving spots or putting a design on right? Wait until I see him; will I give him the raspberries.

Now to tell you a little of what is going on. Now that the Japaneezers have surrendered we are working on our base getting straightened out for it is a new base and there is a lot of work. However when I have a full day off I go to a small village about three quarters of an hour's walk through the mud where I spend the day with a family I made friends with. They are very happy to have us come up. They don't have anything like our children have—no toys, candy or cakes—and when we bring them some small thing it is just like a Christmas to them. They are a very clean, simple-living, honest and religious people. They don't have a church and it's too far out of the way for a priest to go there, especially now that things are still unsettled, but they have a small chapel which they named "Capella di San Rocco." It is small and now they are trying to raise funds to build a larger one by running dances in town. On Sunday morning the people go there and say their rosary, and during the week they stop in and say a prayer. Every night the little oil lamp is lighted and if you see it at night it looks like a guiding light and haven for the traveler just as you read about in the old days. Every evening they say the "Angelus." How these people would appreciate a church while in our land we have many and neglect to use them. With all their hardships they never have forgotten God; we could learn from them.

Now I am waiting and hoping something turns up [so] that I can get home again, so for the present I send my usual love to Mother and Daddy, and a million hugs and kisses for you.

Uncle Johnny

. . .

Maj. Louise R. Camden was single and enlisted in the Army Nurses Corps in 1942 at the age of thirty-eight. Please see Part II: Religious Support and Strength for additional biographical information.

[Excerpt]

[Letter to Martha, Louise's friend, from Camp Bowie on adjusting to military life]

19 Sep 43

. . . . Listen old bean, I'm going to have myself a time—nobody— and I mean nobody is going to have a chance to tell me what to do or when to do it—for at least 2 months after I leave the Army. I'm going someplace where I can eat when I want, and what I want, drink whatever I can find, and sleep until I'm ready to get up. Now if you know of some place like that—besides having no gates with guards, no taps or reveille, no band playing at 6 AM with the sound of marching feet, no uniforms, no salute. . . . almost forgot, it has to have a rocking chair.

LETTER CREDITS

Letter of Rottenfuehrer (Squad Leader) Erik Andersen reprinted courtesy of Kris Dunn.

Letter of P.F.C. Andrew Martin Archer reprinted courtesy of his daughters Betty Archer-Hopkins and Linda Archer.

Letters of Lt. Lucille Backemeyer and Lt. Marvin C. Weber reprinted courtesy of Doris Weber McCallister.

Extracts from the Douglas family publication "Battles Long Ago: Wartime Letters of Dr. R. A. Douglas" reprinted courtesy of the Douglas Family.

Letter of Lt. Walter Best reprinted courtesy of Dr. Harold Thomas.

Letter of P.F.C. Edwin L. Blanche reprinted courtesy of the family of Edwin L. Blanche.

Letters of Maj. Howard "Hitch" Brigham reprinted courtesy of the collection of Robert C. Flint.

Letter of SN1 Jack Burgeman reprinted courtesy of Jack Burgeman.

Letter of Elizabeth Burke reprinted courtesy of Jean Niles.

Letter of F.S. Jim Cahir reprinted courtesy of Jim Cahir in memory of F.S. Patrick Edwards.

Excerpts from letters from Maj. Louise R. Camden reprinted from the collection of Maj. Louise R. Camden courtesy of Richard S. Camden.

Letters of Cpt. A. E. Care reprinted courtesy of Maj. A. E. Care.

Letter of Cpt. Cyril Charters reprinted courtesy of Eileen M. Charters.

Letter of Lt. Lawson Corley, reprinted courtesy of Lt. Lawson Corley, Museum of Authentic Indian Artifacts and War Relics.

Letter of Sgt. Bill Donofrio reprinted courtesy of Sgt. Bill Donofrio.

Letter of Eugene E. Eckstam, M.D., reprinted courtesy of Eugene E. Eckstam, M.D.

Letter of Mary Edith Engle reprinted courtesy of Nancy Engle Gordon.

Letter of Sgt. Charles William Owen Erwood reprinted courtesy of Sally Erwood Carryer.

Letters of Cpt. Franklin M. Elliott reprinted courtesy of De Ronda Elliott.

Letter of Lt. Jennis "Jack" Strickland reprinted from *Red Roses and Silver Wings: A WW II Memoir* by Kitty Strickland Shore, AAM Press P.O. Box 15175, Chevy Chase, M.D. 20825.

Letters of Sgt. Clifford Tompkins reprinted courtesy of the private collection of Marie B. Hardin. All copyrights reserved.

Letter of Fielding D. Tucker reprinted courtesy of Fielding D. Tucker.

Letter of Lt. Joel Vicars Henderson, Jr., reprinted courtesy of his daughter Vicki Jung.

Letter of David James Weepers reprinted courtesy of Donna Niewinski.

Letter of Sgt. J. E. Williams reprinted courtesy of Bruce Williams.

Letters of Lt. Col. H. Paul Wolfe reprinted courtesy of Cynthia V. Wolfe.

Letters of Lt. Clarence Eugene Zieske and Lt. Vernon Lloyd Zieske reprinted courtesy of the private collection of Joseph Mack Zieske Ormond.

Letter of Lt. Wallace Zosel reprinted courtesy of his son Roger Zosel O'Brien.